JEDWARD
OUR STORY

WITH JENNIFER O'BRIEN

JOHN BLAKE

Published by John Blake Publishing Ltd,
3 Bramber Court, 2 Bramber Road,
London W14 9PB, England

www.johnblakepublishing.co.uk

First published in paperback in 2010

ISBN: 978 1 84358 335 6

British Library Cataloguing-in-Publication Data:

A catalogue record for this book is available from the British Library.

Design by www.envydesign.co.uk

Printed in Great Britain by CPI Mackays, Chatham, ME5 8TD

3 5 7 9 10 8 6 4 2

Papers used by John Blake Publishing are natural, recyclable
products made from wood grown in sustainable forests.
The manufacturing processes conform to the environmental
regulations of the country of origin.

CONTENTS

ABOUT THE AUTHOR

Jennifer O'Brien is Showbiz Correspondent for the *Irish Sun* newspaper, which is based in Dublin. She has been a journalist at the paper since 2007, having been recruited by the team as a features/TV writer after completing an MA in Journalism at the National University of Ireland, Galway. Within a year Jennifer, 26, was appointed Showbiz Correspondent and began covering the biggest stories in Ireland and the UK. A regular on Irish TV shows documenting the lives of celebrities, this is her début biography.

acknowledgements

I would like to thank the two and only John and Edward Grimes for the hours of fun and hilarious one-liners – 'Peace out, you guys!' To Louis Walsh for his constant support and Liam McKenna for giving me so much access to the boys and letting me join in their incredible journey.

To my fantastic family, who topped me up with food, advice and support: I love you Mam, Daddy, Jason and Tony.

Also, a huge thank you to my bosses at the *Irish Sun* – editor Michael McNiffe, deputy editor Paul Clarkson and news editors Damien Lane and Neil Cotter for being so accommodating and allowing me flexibility and time to complete the project.

To Chris Doyle and Aoife Redmond for help with photographs.

And last, but by no means least, thanks to my agent Yvonne Kinsella at Prizeman & Kinsella, who has been a guiding light throughout.

Thank you all and long live the Jedward phenomenon.

Foreword

BY LOUIS WALSH

Jedward's manager and
X Factor judge

The first day that I came across John and Edward Grimes is not something I'm likely to forget. We were sitting in the theatre in Glasgow in the summer of 2009 waiting for something exciting to happen. One by one the hopefuls came in. There had been the usual trail of boring and so-so acts and we were beginning to get tired and restless; we needed something new, something different and something fresh.

Enter John and Edward, with their spiky hair, great dress sense and a self-confidence we hadn't seen that day. Simon thought they were cocky – I thought they were hilarious. The moment I looked at John and Edward, I knew the kids were going to love them. They had something that I saw in them from the very start, and of course, Simon claimed this was just because they were from Dublin. It wasn't – I'm not even from Dublin. I could see they had something and I liked their attitude.

Whatever the X factor is, I was sure that John and Edward had it beneath the surface. When it came to the boot-camp stages of the show, the boys really shone. They took no prisoners in the audition stages and showed us all that they were serious about getting through.

From the beginning, I could see they were charmers and they had Cheryl and Dannii in the palms of their hands at the first audition. The whirlwind really began when I got to mentor the groups for the show and John and Edward came to Italy for the final selections. We had a hard time choosing which groups we were going to go with and Ronan Keating really wasn't keen on putting John and Edward through. I just had a feeling, though – and I went with it.

It turned out to be one of the best decisions I have ever made on the show. From week to week, John and Edward entertained like no other contestants and made the show their own. Everywhere I went, people were asking me about them – they began to take over the whole thing. No matter what the judges might say, no one could wait to see what they had for us every week.

Behind the scenes I got to know the boys and they were so hard-working and just enjoying every minute of their newfound fame. At the same time, a lot of people were beginning to give them a hard time. I have to say I was passionate about sticking up for John and Edward, and full of admiration for the way they handled everything. They were two kids who were just following their dream and people everywhere were crazy about them. I told them not to let the ones who were giving them a tough time get them down – and they didn't.

I've been in this industry for over 30 years and John and Edward experienced more in their first few months in the limelight than most acts do in 10 years. There was barely a day when they were not on the front of the newspaper. I knew I had made the right decision and I think Simon knew that, too.

Of course when it all came to an end I was sad to see them leave the show. People had been asking me whether I was going to manage them or not and I began to think seriously about it. Even though I still had lots going on with Westlife and my new girl band Wonderland, I couldn't pass up the opportunity to work with John and Edward. They had something special and I knew they were not just going to fade into oblivion like so many *X Factor* acts had in the past. I decided that I wanted to work with them full time and it was a decision I have not come to regret.

Before long, there were not enough days in the week for all the calls we were getting about the boys. Liam McKenna was appointed as their tour manager and from the start they had a brilliant team around to look after them. From the beginning of 2010, John and Edward were literally booked out for months ahead. There were offers from all of the TV shows in the UK and Ireland – everyone wanted to have them on.

John and Edward were on *The Late Late Toy Show*, *Graham Norton*, *Jonathan Ross* and *Sky News* – there are just too many shows to mention and everywhere they went, besotted fans were following their every move. It was a phenomenon I hadn't seen in years: I knew they were going to have to get a record and an album out, and that they would sell like hotcakes.

I told them they were really going to have to work hard if they wanted to make the most of things and they never once complained because they just love what they are doing so much. Before long, we had Vanilla Ice on board for 'Ice Ice Baby', which topped the charts.

Everything just fell into place for the boys. Even when we parted ways with Sony, Universal were eager to get them on board and we got working on an album straight away. I knew the record companies would all want to work with the boys: they are different – young, exciting and full of energy. Who wouldn't get a good feeling out of managing them?

When *Planet Jedward* came out, it sold more in Ireland in its first week than any other record had done all year. Kids were going into music stores and buying records once again and that's the main thing John and Edward have done for the industry – they have made kids love getting their hands on records again. They have been the boost that the record industry in Ireland needed and, one year on, their name is still on everyone's lips. There's no mistaking John and Edward, and they are recognised everywhere they go. I think they have a fantastic career ahead of them and could turn their hands to anything, from TV presenting to modelling.

Everyone that the boys have worked with, from record companies to fast food giants, comes back to me to say that they just want to work with John and Edward again. It's their positive attitude that has made them more successful than other people who were on the show. They are always in the right frame of mind and they always deliver – they are everything a pop star is meant to be.

Another thing I have noticed is that they haven't let it all affect them. Things could really have gone to their heads but John and Edward have remained true to themselves. Right from the very first day on the show, they never altered who they are for anybody: they are the genuine article and not prepared to compromise.

Working with Jedward has brought so much of the fun factor back into my job. It really reminds me of the early days with Boyzone and Westlife back in the 1990s. The mania that follows them everywhere they go really is something to see and I love to see John and Edward get on the road and tour all around Ireland. It's like a new lease of life and there's pandemonium wherever they go. Too many bands don't even want to do the local gigs anymore, but I know just how important that is for a loyal fanbase. John and Edward would go to the ends of the earth for their fans: I have never seen an act return the devotion the fans give like the boys. Even when they close the door on the world after an 18-hour day, they are straight on the Internet to leave messages and chat to their followers.

And it isn't something they're trying to do out of self-promotion – they genuinely adore their fans and want to talk to them and hear their feedback. I just don't think there's another act out there today with an attitude like that. I thought they could be big, but never knew just how big they might actually get to be. I'm very proud of them and if we find anything half as exciting as Jedward on this year's show then I think I will be happy.

One thing is for sure, though – we will never find another John and Edward. They are truly unique and that's what makes them so successful. Kids in America will go crazy for these guys and it just gets more and more exciting. My phone never stops ringing with people wanting to book them and long may it continue.

Jedward are two of the nicest guys that you could meet and as long as they are still having fun, I think we will have them around for a long time to come.

preFace

by Jennifer O'Brien

Back in the summer of 2009 I received word that a set of twins from Dublin were causing a stir on *The X Factor*. With nothing to go on but the fact that they were identical and into singing, I spent hours on the Internet trying to discover their identity.

Eventually I stumbled across a website about the Grimes brothers, aka John and Edward. After a quick read, I decided it had to be those two adorable-looking brothers who were the talk of the show. I was right but I had no idea how much of the next year would be spent writing article after article documenting the schoolboys' rise to fame.

After revealing that students John and Edward Grimes were through to the boot-camp stages of the 2009 series, I set about finding out as much as possible about them. Before long, we had tracked down their Lucan home, chatted with their beloved grandfather Kevin and pals from the estate where they lived. Little did I know then that one year on the pair would be the most famous twins in Ireland and the UK.

As the series began to air on ITV1 and TV3 one thing became clear: John and Edward were becoming two of the most talked-about contestants that *The X Factor* had ever produced. In every newsroom in Ireland and the UK the race was on to get the best stories about the boys. Reporters were dispatched to come to Dublin and find out everything they could about John and Edward. Just as the boys were fast becoming television gold, they were also gold in terms of newspaper stories – the public could not get enough of the quiff-haired duo.

When people began to get nasty towards the Irish boys, I couldn't help but feel for them. There they were, two young boys on their own in the UK facing constant abuse from the public. But over in Ireland, we needn't have worried: John and Edward were made of sterner stuff and sailed above all the haters to win their way into the hearts of people everywhere.

I sat backstage at *The X Factor* on the fateful night in November 2009 when Simon Cowell allowed the vote to go to the public and Lucie Jones was sent home. The masses seemed to turn on John, Edward and Simon but from that night onwards I loved the boys even more.

They were visibly shaken as they came back to Louis' dressing room and hugged their parents, John and Susanna, saying how bad they felt that they had been saved and poor Lucie was being sent home. Behind all of the booing and cheering were two young boys who had feelings just like everybody else. That day, I saw that John and Edward were so much more than a novelty act on a TV show: they were two very unique teens with hearts of absolute gold. They sailed through six weeks on the show before eventually being voted off and many believe that if voting lines had been open in Ireland then John and Edward could have won the entire show.

But it didn't really matter because the boys have gone on to become the most successful and most-loved contestants of the series by a long mile. I was to spend late 2009 and most of 2010 following John and Edward on the biggest journey of their lives. The boys have worked non-stop, with tours of Ireland, the UK, two hit singles, a number one album and two TV shows; they have managed to squeeze more into one year than most people manage in a lifetime.

And the most heart-warming thing is that underneath it all, they are the exact same John and Edward that we all saw walking onto the stage in front of the judges last summer. There are no diva demands, no strops and welcoming smiles for everyone they meet. John and Edward have what so many modern acts lack and that is complete and utter devotion to their fans. Whether it's the early hours of the morning or late at light, their primary concern is keeping in touch with their legions of followers. Jedward know their fans are the reason why they are where they are today and they're willing to return that love in spades. They never tire of posing for photographs or signing autographs and their constantly happy demeanour is the reason why they have survived and thrived.

Having since learnt of the hard time they endured at school, the twins' remarkable personalities are all the more admirable. Both opened up like never before about their experience at the hands of bullies and I'm sure their tale of triumph will be a huge boost to many school-goers reading this book. John and Edward are a credit to their parents John and Susanna, brother Kevin James and extended family and friends. They are also an asset to manager Louis Walsh, tour manager Liam McKenna and the entire X *Factor* team who got them where they are today. At just 18 years old, they are two of the most professional artists I have ever seen in the world of showbiz and they give every single gig 100 per cent.

Documenting the thus-far short but eventful lives of Ireland's most famous twins has been an absolute pleasure and I would happily spend every day on the road with the hilarious Jedward. Much as I will miss writing about them, however, I have a feeling the journey of the Grimes twins is still only just beginning.

Chapter One

In The Beginning...

FOR THOUSANDS OF fans it might be hard to imagine a world without John and Edward Grimes but until 1991, that's the way it was. Susanna and John Grimes were living with their toddler son Kevin in Celbridge. While John worked in computers, Susanna worked in a nearby school.

The couple were thrilled to learn that they were expecting twins in late 1991 – their little family would now be complete; all going well, two bundles of joy were set to arrive just before Christmas. In true Jedward style, the twins made a dramatic and unannounced entrance into the world two months ahead of schedule. On 13 October, at 31 weeks into her pregnancy, Susanna was rushed to hospital with a stomach virus and told that her babies were in danger. Despite efforts by doctors at Dublin's Rotunda hospital to stall a premature delivery, John and Edward were determined to make their dramatic entrance into the world. Weighing just 4 lbs and 5 lbs respectively, John and Edward were whisked away to the neo-natal unit.

The gorgeous tots spent weeks in an incubator and grew stronger and stronger with each day that passed. Both John and Edward still thank God that they survived and sometimes they think about the fact that they might not be here at all.

'We know that we are lucky to be alive because we were born two months early,' John says. 'Maybe that is one of the reasons why we are so close because we spent all that time in the womb and then went on this journey together. We were tiny babies and had to stay beside each other in the one incubator for weeks before they allowed our parents to take us home.'

Edward agrees: 'They say that twins have a unique bond and I think ours is really strong. We were fighters from the beginning. We were born against the odds, survived against the odds, and now we live our lives fighting against the odds.'

After their fame started to grow on *X Factor*, the lads became an inspiration for premature babies all over the world. John and Edward have been added to a list of 'Famous Premmie Babies' on a number of online sites and they take pride of place alongside a number of very well known figures throughout the world such as Albert Einstein, Stevie Wonder and Mark Twain.

'I think that when you are born premature you have the instinct to survive that other people don't have,' John shrugs. 'Maybe that's why we are always running around the place because we spent weeks at the beginning of our lives in an incubator, sleeping and growing. Our mom had our older brother, Kevin, at 28 weeks and she always says she was blessed to have us, her three little miracles.

'I was the first to be allowed home,' adds John with a grin, 'because I was 10 minutes older.'

Edward arrived home a week later, 'Much to the confusion of our older brother,' laughs Edward.

The boys have no shortage of memories from their early years and love to talk about the mischief that they got up to. John begins: 'From an early age me and Edward loved to draw, we had two colouring boxes which were shaped like teddy bears. We loved to use our crayons and markers, especially on the walls in our house.'

Like a lot of twins, John and Edward developed their own language. 'We used to call a radiator a "heater-radtor" and a pancake a "panacake",' Edward laughs.

As well as being close to their mom, dad and brother, the twins are very close to other members of their family, in particular their granny Susan and their granddad Kevin who passed away in August 2010.

'We spent a lot of time in our grandparents' house. We used to love heading off to school every morning in granddad's car. He would play country music and we would sing along to it.'

Edward says: 'At Halloween we had massive bonfires – we were lucky that the fire brigade never arrived at our grandparents' home.'

John interrupts: 'One of our earliest memories is when we got our first dog, Trixie. She had been abandoned outside the gates of Dublin Zoo – this was the beginning of our love for dogs. Every night before we went to bed we would say a prayer for our dogs.

'Our granddad built us a tree house, as climbing trees was one of our favourite things to do. I remember John falling out of a tree when he was five but like a cat he landed on his feet and started to climb it again.'

The boys were into anything and everything that would entertain their sense of adventure outdoors – they rarely spent time inside. Edward says: 'We loved being outside and at one with nature. The thing about me and John is, we never really got into the whole TV thing – although we loved Disney programmes. From an early age we were very creative and imaginative. We made clay pots and plates and insisted that our mom bake them in the oven. She did it to keep us happy.'

Their mother was always trying to educate them to exercise caution if any strangers came up to talk to them while they were outside playing. 'When we were younger, our mom used to scare the life out of us with the whole "stranger danger" thing,' John says. 'She gave us this stranger danger book at one stage and it just freaked us out – we certainly never talked to strangers after she read it to us.'

'One Christmas, we got Furbies from Santa, but we were actually very frightened of them and at night we thought they were going to come to life so we locked them away in our toy chest.'

The twins used to let their imagination run into overdrive after their mom put them to bed when they were toddlers. 'Monsters were everywhere,' Edward giggles. 'We would lie in our beds and imagine that the characters from

Pokémon were coming to life and that we were the Pokémon masters.

'I remember that we used get freaked out by our clothes hanging in the wardrobe because we imagined they looked like people in the dark of the night. Then we would put our blankets over our heads and giggle.'

The adorable boys were bundles of energy as they grew up and loved nothing better than getting out into the fresh air to play. Edward is full of memories of hanging out in his granddad Kevin's garden every day. He says: 'I remember our granddad used to go out on his tractor to cut grass for the local GAA club and bring our older brother Kevin with him. We thought Kevin was the coolest kid. We were allowed help granddad on his ride-on lawnmower.'

Edward narrowly avoided injuring himself when he decided to take the family's ride-on lawnmower for a spin. 'I got on it and figured out how to start it and then I crashed into the neighbour's hedge,' he laughs.

The boys made their own fun with various things that their grandparents had hanging around outside the house. And usually Edward was the butt of jokes played on him by John. 'John put me inside a wheel barrow once and left me there for ages. That wasn't cool, it really freaked me out.'

John and Edward became animal lovers from a very early age and were keen to have a selection of pets. 'Me and Edward's house is a loud and busy place with our family and friends coming and going. We have dogs, cats and we had a pet budgie – his name was Joey but he died the same day as our granddad passed away.'

John and Edward's favourite cartoons when they were younger were *Bugs Bunny*, *Top Cat*, *Tom and Jerry*, *Scooby Doo*, *Rugrats*, *Recess*, *Pokémon* and *The Simpsons*. The lads continued to watch these cartoons when they got older, even though some of their friends were into *South Park*. 'We didn't want to watch things like that because that cartoon is for adults,' John says. 'On Saturday mornings we would go downstairs wrapped in our duvets and tune in to our favourite Disney channel.'

One summer's day, when the boys were feeling particularly mischievous, they decided to play hide and seek on their parents. They positioned themselves under a car in their drive and waited to be found. 'Our parents were freaking out because they didn't know where we were,' Edward remembers. 'As we were only three, they thought we had been taken. After that day, a double lock was placed on the front door to avoid a similar incident happening again.'

Another day, John and Edward were in their back garden in Celbridge and decided to climb the wall at the rear of the house. From there, they spotted a group of children doing something that they had not witnessed before. The kids seemed to be 'floating on wheely shoes,' according to Edward. 'That was the first time we saw roller blades and we ran into our mom and screamed that we wanted them. Christmas was coming and, in our letter to Santa, we put roller blades at the top of our wish list. On Christmas morning I got red roller blades and John got black ones. We had a couple of falls but after a lot of practice we became pros.'

in THe Beginning...

The twins started primary school at five years old and admit that they didn't really mind going. 'We used to like school, particularly art and P.E.,' Edward says. 'Both of us would always be waiting for playtime. We were always together – we didn't want the teacher putting us apart and even if she did, we would end up talking to one another across the room.'

John and Edward always remember their home as a clean and tidy one and say that their mother encouraged them to keep their room tidy. 'Our parents like to keep the house clean, but we aren't like that. We realise that a house cannot be clean all the time. We don't mind when people come around and everything is a bit messy. At the moment, we are so busy with our work we find it difficult to get around to cleaning our rooms.'

The boys become emotional when they remember their late granddad Kevin and the fun they used to have with him as children. 'I remember when he bought us our first pony. We called him Dusty, do you remember that, John?' Edward asks. 'I know that might sound posh, but Dusty was a pony that had been rescued. He had been treated badly during his early life. We enjoyed training him and encouraging him to go over jumps by placing food on the other side of the jumps – and it worked!' Edward exclaims.

'Our granddad was amazing and he was our hero.'

The boys were also taught some DIY by their granddad and put it to use. Edward says: 'When we were younger, we decided to put an extension on our treehouse and we painted the whole treehouse. It was the best one around when we were small.'

John adds: 'We had our little tree house but we wanted a whole street to ourselves. From an early age we wanted to buy a street and call it John and Edward Street and have all our family move in to it. Our dream was to have a Neverland ranch like Michael Jackson's. Me and John would love to have a monument of ourselves – just like the Egyptians. But we would need to employ loads of people to build it.'

'We are going to prove to people that they need to build this monument while we are alive and not when we are dead, so they need to appreciate us now,' laughs Edward.

John and Edward's first best friends came in the form of two puppies they found near the Curragh race course in Co. Kildare. 'These puppies were beagles and we taught them tricks,' Edward says. 'John's dog was called Lassie and my dog was called Lucky – until I realised that calling a dog Lucky wasn't a good move. The dog died suddenly and I was very upset. Mom bought me a robo dog, but it couldn't replace Lucky. Lassie is still alive aged 12 – or 84 in dog years. She doesn't look her age!'

This lesson in the harsh reality of owning pets was to prepare John and Edward for losing many of their animals throughout the years. As previously mentioned, just before this book went to print, the boys were mourning the loss of their beloved budgie Joey. Edward says: 'We had this budgie for nine years and he was always there in the background tweeting away. We loved him and taught him to do tricks – he even starred in his own video on our YouTube channel, JedwardTV. He was like this funky little bird and was one of the family. He often sat on one of our shoulders and he loved to hang out there. We were sad when Joey passed away, but he will be remembered as this superstar bird on our Twitter. He had many fans.'

When they think about being younger, John and Edward's train of thought swings from school to playing to eating. John says: 'When we were in baby infants, there was this kid who stuck peas up his nose. Then he put crayons in and we didn't know what the hell was going on. If we were bored in school we used to draw pictures on our desks when the teacher wasn't looking.'

Edward interrupts: 'We also had this swing set and we used to swing so high on it – we would be full on in the air and about to go into heaven. We used it as monkey bars as well, so it was a full-on agility camp in our own garden.

'We weren't really loud as kids. We used to draw loads and loads of cool pictures. We used to see kids when we were really young in school having temper tantrums but me and John used to think, what's the problem? You would never see us in the corner screaming and shouting and having temper tantrums, we were too busy having fun.'

When the boys moved house, they were told that they could have their own rooms for the very first time. Parents Susanna and John thought that this would be music to John and Edward's ears. But even back then, the twins hated to be parted.

Edward says: 'I remember moving into our second house and we were told that we could have a room each but we just decided to move into the same room. Our parents gave us all separate rooms. I had my own, John had his own and Kevin had his own room. On the first night of moving in, we all sat in this massive bed with all these teddy bears. I moved up to John's room and we got bunk beds and that was really cool.'

Whenever John and Edward wanted an adventure, they would hop on their bicycles and hit the road. Sometimes they didn't even tell their poor mum where they were going. 'We used to just hop on the bikes and head down the road,' John laughs. 'We would be there laughing our heads off but then we knew that we were going to get in loads of trouble on our return. We often got punctures, so we went through lots of cycling kits, but we became record breakers in fixing punctures. It was really cool to be able to fix our bikes and cycle everywhere.

'I want to tell all the kids who are reading this book right now that they should get up and go out there and have fun,' says John. 'Cycle a bike or run or jump, but don't sit in front of a computer all day long. That is such a waste of time – there's no point in playing video games of soccer when you can go outside to play the real thing.'

John and Edward went on many holidays with their family right up until they were 18, but have fond memories of their holidays in Ireland with their grandparents. On one occasion, they found themselves in a bed and breakfast in Wexford where John took a tumble and fell against a window.

'He wasn't really hurt too bad so that was OK,' Edward shrugs. 'It was one of our favourite holidays because we got to go fishing on the beach. I remember that week we caught loads of flat fish and I wanted to bring them all home and put them in an aquarium. Our brother Kevin went out and bought an aquarium and we still have it at home which is cool.'

On another family outing, John and Edward found themselves in Cavan near the north of Ireland to visit relatives of their granny. Both boys would be strapped safely into the back of the car and entertained themselves on long journeys by singing their favourite songs and playing 'I Spy'. On this trip to Cavan, they were overwhelmed to find themselves on a large farm with acres of land for them to explore.

John says: 'We were running all around the fields and having so much fun – it was like we had never been that free before and you could run and run without bumping into anything because there was nothing there.'

Disaster soon struck when older brother Kevin lost his footing and fell down a well while they were playing. 'That was really scary and the grown-ups had to come and pull Kevin out of the well.'

Edward says: 'It was really freaky because it wasn't one of those massive wells – it was more like a hole in the ground and when he fell in he just disappeared, we didn't know what was happening, but thankfully he was quickly rescued by our cousin, Matt.

'There were chickens everywhere too, we tried to capture them and get pictures with them.'

On another trip to a friend of their mother's who lived on a farm, John and Edward discovered sheep for the first time and wanted to take one home as a pet. John remembers: 'I just thought they were the coolest-looking things with their woolly coats and we begged our mom to let us take one home, but she had to say no, and we refused to eat lamb after that.'

The boys would spend hours and hours playing outside with older brother Kevin and loved to collect acorns and chestnuts with him. From an early age, their granddad had taught them the names of all of the plants in his Dublin garden. John and Edward can remember picking home-grown rhubarb with their granny and helping her to make rhubarb tarts in the kitchen.

They can also recall getting down on their hands and knees and attempting to cut the whole lawn with scissors. 'It took forever,' John giggles. 'And then our granddad said to us that the lawnmower was down in the shed.'

The boys loved spending Christmas in their grandparents' house and can recall the excitement of waiting for Santa to come. Edward says, 'I can remember that every year around Christmas, our granny would give us our granddad's wellies and we would put on loads of pairs of his socks and go outside into the snow. Every single Christmas, when it was cold outside, we would throw water outside of the door to make an ice-rink. It was like in *Home Alone*, when the little boy put all of the water on the steps. The result was that we got in a lot of trouble because visitors often slipped on it. On one occasion it happened to our dad and he wasn't very happy.'

John and Edward liken their young selves to Dennis the Menace and can remember kicking up a fuss when they were taken for their very first haircut. 'The first time that we went to get our hair cut was a really, really weird moment,' John recalls. 'I remember that day. We ran around the hairdresser like lunatics and there was a guy with a pair of scissors running around after us trying to get us to sit down. We just didn't want to get it done. I think that even back then when we were children, we loved our hair and didn't want to cut it off. Finally, after hours of running around, we got it cut. I think that's a really stressful point for all kids because you are small and your hair is growing and then someone comes along who wants to hack it all off and that seems weird.'

The cute blonde boys admit that their hair started to get a little darker as they got older. 'It was naturally blonde, though,' John insists.

Their fear of hairdressers also extends to dentists. John can remember their very first visit to get their teeth checked out. As with hospital appointments, trips to the hairdresser and clothes shopping, John and Edward were always taken to see the dentist together.

'It was really weird because we got fissure seals on our teeth,' John recalls. 'It was really scary because movies always terrify you about going to the dentist. It turned out that our dentist was OK and said we had no cavities or anything and we had healthy teeth.'

While John and Edward are still blessed with healthy teeth, they insist that they will never go down the road of getting veneers or surgery to achieve that perfect Hollywood smile. 'I just like when teeth don't look perfect and I think that it gives you character,' John says. 'We like our teeth just the way that they are and it helps people to tell us apart from one another too.'

They are keen to stay talking about their playful

childhood and John says, 'In our first house, we used to have loads and loads of rose bushes out in our front garden, there were many different colours and then we moved house and took them with us.

'The first cat that we had wasn't officially our cat, but it was the next-door neighbour's cat and we kind of adopted him. We called him Felix and left out saucers of milk for him each morning.

'One of our favourite soft toys was a huge blue rabbit thing that myself and Edward were totally mad about.'

Edward adds: 'John broke the window in our house with a football more than once and our neighbours were always really worried that we would break one of their windows with our football antics. Windows did get broken, but we were not the culprits!'

John concludes the story of the boys' childhood by saying: 'We were never superstitious when we were kids at all but we don't like to see one magpie on its own. When people say that a bird pooing on you is good luck – I mean it clearly isn't, it's clearly bad luck'

Chapter two
SCHOOLDAYS

BOTH JOHN AND EDWARD clearly remember being shipped off with their lunchboxes for their first day at school. The adorable twins were just 5 years old as they held their parents' hands and walked through the school gates. There were no tears from John and Edward as they left their parents and walked into junior infants because they had one another.

'We were always side by side,' John shrugs. 'We had our little lunchboxes and went into our first primary school.'

The twins would find themselves in and out of a couple of different primary schools, but didn't mind being on the move. And wherever they found themselves, they always had big brother Kevin to protect them.

Even when they were children, there were no bad foods in the lunchboxes of health-conscious John and Edward. 'I remember all of the other kids had lots of sweet things. We used to have home-made brown bread with healthy fillings,' Edward says. 'We would bring drinks like milk or juice – we didn't have fancy things in our lunchboxes that were gimmicky. From a young age we loved fruit.

The twins admit that, from their very first day in primary school, they were always up to mischief. With inquisitive little minds and lots of energy to burn up, both John and Edward were keen to keep their teachers on their toes. Edward recalls: 'I remember we had a teacher that we called Ms Crayon because we could not pronounce her name correctly. She used to take our toys off of us when we weren't behaving and myself and John would sneak back into the classroom to make sure they were not lonely.'

It was in primary school that the boys had their first experience of how mean other children could be when one girl began to throw her milk at them. 'She was in our class but now, looking back at it, I think it was one of those puppy love things where she was secretly trying to get our attention – but we would never do things like that to other people,' Edward says.

Neither John nor Edward would ever venture into the school grounds if their other half wasn't feeling up to it that day. John laughs, 'If one of us woke up and the other was sick, then we would know that we were going to have a day off. We always kind of got sick together because we were always with each other.'

The boys moved to a second primary school. They made their way through Junior and Senior Infants and soon found themselves preparing for their First Holy Communion in First Class. They didn't know it then but that First Communion day was to be the first of Edward's many performances in front of a live audience. While standing at the back of the church, before the ceremony took place, the seven-year-old discovered a microphone and couldn't resist the urge to speak. He laughs: 'I took hold of it and said something like "How's everybody doing out there?" My teacher wasn't very happy and I got in trouble. Lots of people laughed and I thought that it was funny.'

Because they were identical twins, the lads were always getting a lot of attention from outsiders. Mum Susanna dressed them in similar outfits and they got many 'oohs' and 'aahs' from passers by as they walked around town holding her hand.

'*The Limerick Leader* printed a photo of us wearing identical sweatshirts when we were 3. It had been taken by our aunt, Miriam, who entered it for a photographic competition and won first place. Our mom says she was asked to let the three of us do child modelling but she decided that it would put too much pressure on us at a young age.'

John adds that, although they both tried hard to concentrate at school, the lads preferred to express themselves through art and music from a young age. 'We weren't these students who were like, amazing,' John shrugs. 'We were always pretending that we knew what the teacher was talking about, even when we didn't. I think that we were just like normal kids. We weren't nerds but just thought, what are we doing here?'

As the years passed by in primary school, John and Edward continued to stick together and never really became part of a huge group of friends. Both of the lads feel that this was because they preferred each other's company to anyone else's and were shy around strangers.

'You always have this group of people that think that they are really cool but we were never really one of them,' Edward explains. 'One thing that used to keep us happy was doing loads and loads of art and I remember drawing the whole layout of the school on a piece of tissue paper which my mom decided to frame.'

While in primary school, they also turned to running as a way to keep them out of mischief. The twins soon learned that if they were part of the running team, they could get some time out of class and escape and run should they find themselves on detention.

At the end of each day, the boys ran home happy that they had made it through another day of school. John grins: 'Sometimes I wouldn't have my homework done, and I would say that I couldn't find it. I'd then do it during class and hand it up and be like, "Hey, I found it!"

'We were never pressured by our mom and dad to do our homework or put under pressure when we were in primary school. My favourite subject was art because you could do all of these different things and I used to like maths but I was never really any good at it.'

Edward interrupts, 'I used to like maths too – until it got really hard.'

When the twins were just 6 years old, John was given a guitar and Edward found himself the proud owner of a new violin. A love of music soon developed as the lads swapped around their instruments and found themselves jamming with older brother Kevin, who played the drums.

They also started singing and mimicking their favourite artists from the radio. 'We liked to listen to The Spice Girls and Boyzone and people like that,' Edward says.

'One thing that we want to make clear is that we were not stage-school kids, but we think it is a fun way to learn how to sing and dance with kids of your own age.'

John modestly adds: 'We just did everything ourselves – we never even practise, maybe we should start practising and we could get a lot better.'

In the privacy of their small bedroom, the youngsters would line up their first-ever audience in the form of their favourite cuddly toys. 'Our teddies used to watch us and we would sing and dance for them,' John giggles. 'We had these little concerts for them or we would go into the bathroom where there was a really good echo, like a microphone. Hairbrushes were our microphones and we would sing to our dogs too.'

Both the lads joined the school choir at an early age and loved to sing along with their classmates while at school. 'I remember the first video we ever saw was NSYNC's "Bye Bye Bye" and we were just amazed,' recalls Edward. 'We had been watching *Recess* and switched over and we were like, "Oh my God, this is so cool."'

The lads soon developed a love of Backstreet Boys songs and music video channels, and they spent all of their time singing. 'We just liked performing and loved Britney Spears, NSYNC and Justin Timberlake,' John says. 'I think that every kid wants to be a pop star and we were always more interested in pop than in work.'

When the boys were 12 years old, it was decided that they would attend a boarding school on the outskirts of Dublin. Neither John nor Edward fully knew what to expect from the experience but thought that it was going to be like something out of the movies. The boys packed up and left their family home in Kildare to spend their first nights away from home at the fee-paying school.

Edward says: 'I think with me and John, we kind of thought that boarding school would be like it is in *Harry Potter*, with feasts and magic and all of that. We thought we were going to have owls and cloaks, but it wasn't like that at all.'

From the outset, John and Edward say that they were excited about starting secondary school. 'We came into this dorm and there were another four boys in it,' John recalls. 'I felt like they were apprehensive but me and John were looking forward to making new friends,' he says.

Even as first years, the twins had to endure hours of study classes and attended school on Saturdays. 'We were 12 years old and I think we were so innocent in comparison to some of the other students in our year.'

The twins took comfort in each other's company – away from the peer pressure of some of their other schoolmates. Edward admits that the boys realised they just weren't like some of the students. He says: 'When we were that age, there would be kids cursing and we were just never like that. We never spoke like that and we weren't going to do it just because other people were doing it – what's the point of that? I don't know if people saw us as weird or something but we didn't care.'

But the boys *did* care.

John and Edward were the target of pranks by some of their fellow pupils. Try as they did to shrug it off and put it all down to jealousy, the twins did begin to wonder what it was that made those students act in such a mean way.

'We turned to our mom for advice. She tried to explain to us that people with low self-esteem can become very nasty to others because it makes them feel better about themselves.'

John says he felt like he was missing out on things while at boarding school. 'It was kind of like we weren't in the real world. Going to school on Saturday was hard, but we just got involved in everything.'

John and Edward signed up for sports, drama and music classes to occupy themselves during the school term and to use up some of that energy that they are now so famous for. 'We were involved in cricket and canoeing – everything that we could do in school, we just wanted to get out there and do it,' Edward admits. 'There was also athletics, rugby, and hockey. I think the thing that we missed most in school was just the normality of being at home with our parents. We also missed our pets and our grandparents a lot.'

Edward feels that modern culture and the media have a lot to do with how teenagers think these days. 'I feel like the way movies have gone now are kind of taking away the innocence of kids,' he says. 'They are being exposed to things that they are not emotionally ready for and some of their peer group are encouraging them to do things they are not comfortable with – they do it to look cool.'

While boys in the school became interested in girls,

John and Edward also started getting more and more attention from the female population. Girls obviously fancied the Grimes brothers, but their good looks would come to be a double-edged sword and attract the wrath of some their fellow male students. From their first year in secondary school, John and Edward noticed that girls used to flock to them, but this led to more taunting from some of the other pupils.

The boys know plenty of other people that have been bullied, including some of their fans, who have shared their experiences with them. 'Bullying can start with small things, but everything kind of builds up. People seem to think that there has to be some kind of big scenario but the little things always add up too. Finally, you just have a meltdown and you start crying because you are sick of it. I have learnt that you must always tell an adult what is going on. You always remember the people who were the bullies.'

John adds, 'There was always that certain group in every year who thought they were the cool ones and would pick on certain people – I think that it's like that in every school.'

The twins' striking good looks, athletic build, talent for entertaining and popularity with the girls made them stand out. They both feel that the fact that there was two of them made the situation more difficult. 'It didn't matter what people said to us – we just went and did our thing and got involved in everything that we could get involved in.'

While the boys insist that they never really considered themselves as 'hot', they were never short of offers from the girls. 'There were some girls who would never talk to us then and want to talk to us now, so that's a bit weird.'

Although there would later be reports that the twins were once hung out of the school windows by bullies and put into schoolbags, both John and Edward say these stories are not true. 'In the end we just always did our own thing.'

The twins had their own set of family values and morals instilled from an early age and had absolutely no interest in experimenting with alcohol. The boys' clean-living attitude was again something that set them apart from their peers and made them appear 'strange' to some pupils. But remarkably, both John and Edward stayed true to themselves and believed that their strength to resist peer pressure set them apart from everyone else – in a very good way.

John admits: 'We didn't want that stuff and were cool enough not to have to say "yes" to some people, just like sheep. Because me and Edward thought about things in a different way, that just meant that we had been influenced by different things. It was like certain people had been watching some brainwashing show and we had missed it.'

Now that they are rich and famous, John and Edward are certainly having the last laugh – but they still come into contact with the people who gave them a hard time. As inevitably happens in many cases of bullying, the bullies later want to befriend those they have taunted.

John shrugs: 'I still see them and they could say "hey" to me now and that's kind of funny. I think that everyone is on the same level and there's no reason for people to pick on others.'

The twins dream movie-esque hopes for secondary school never were achieved, but they realise now that they were just that – dreams.

'Everything was meant to be like the movies,' Edward insists. 'We had the bar set high and couldn't wait to have our locker and see how amazing everything was. We thought that it was going to be the soccer team and the cheerleading team. I think that you think it's going to be this big dream.'

And John maintains a philosophical approach to being bullied. 'You have to go through bad things to know when you have good things. You finally get there and the good parts are so good because you have already been through the bad parts and so finally when you get there, it is amazing.'

Looking back, both John and Edward feel that they may have been a bit laid-back about making friends because they always had each other. The twins went through everything together, and became each other's rock during the really difficult times. 'I think that when people are on their own in school, then they have to make friends. But me and Edward didn't really because we always had each other,' John remarks. 'We always knew what the right thing was to do and we never ever did the wrong thing. We never wanted to be like everyone else, we did not want to be clones of other people.'

Edward says: 'I think that everything that has happened to us made us the people we are now. The reason that we were able to go on and do X Factor and take everything that happened to us was because we were determined to defy all our critics. I feel like you learn from every single experience. Life is about learning and moving on.

'There was a story in the newspaper that bullying made us tough, but I think everything makes you tough. It's cool for kids to have a chance to talk to someone outside the home about things that might be getting them down. ChildLine does a lot of important work in this area. I feel kids today are under all this pressure from outside influences and there is pressure to be perfect. Normal for us would be totally weird for someone else and everyone has different experiences. Kids think that things have to be a certain way but real life isn't like that. Now that we are living the dream, sometimes it's not as some kids think it is, but it's cool that they want to be like us.'

One place that the twins were always happy was in music and drama sessions. The lads signed up for every show going in school and were not shy about showcasing their talents in front of the entire student body. The bullies could call John and Edward what they liked, but they were never going to take away their confidence and love of performing.

'Me and Edward were in a variety of school shows. We weren't picked for the lead parts but we still enjoyed being in the chorus line. There are thousands of kids all around Ireland who audition for the Olympia Theatre each year. They may not get a part but I think that they should realise that there is always a way and that they should always have belief in themselves – look at us, we never gave up on our dream. We want to tell people being bullied that there are thousands of people on sites on the Internet who hate me and Edward but we don't care and we do our own thing. I feel like you have got to realise that it's just a little digital world with someone sitting typing things behind a computer and it doesn't matter.'

The boys want victims to stand up to those who hassle them and to stand out from the crowd. 'You don't need to follow everyone else,' Edward insists. 'It's like when you are in school and someone falls and everyone starts laughing just because they think that everyone else is laughing and that's the cool thing to do. That's not the cool thing to do – the cool thing to do is go over and pick that person up.'

John and Edward think that the best way to overcome the bullies is to just keep being the person that you already are and not to allow anyone to make you change.

The pair also had to try to concentrate on their studies and get good grades. They endured hours of study for their Junior Certificate exams when they were 15 but insist that they didn't really stress out about their academic performance. 'We weren't nerds but we liked our subject teachers and tried to do our best.'

John adds: 'Yeah, like we did study lots sometimes and we did all of the same kind of subjects but I can't really remember the exams.'

In 2006, John and Edward decided to enter a talent competition in school. 'All we wanted to do was get up on stage and show people what we could do,' John says. 'I knew that we could show everyone that we were serious about things.'

The twins used to spend hours in their room, practising

their routine and listening to music. When they plucked up the courage to perform in the school show, they tried not to feel the nerves. 'It was great when we got up on stage and heard the music because people started to cheer,' Edward remembers. 'I think that was one of our favourite memories from school.'

With their short dark hair, the boys are barely recognisable on YouTube footage as they take to the stage in front of the entire school. Wearing jeans and jackets, the 15-year-olds look nervous as the girls in the audience scream their heads off for the lads. It's no surprise that 'I Want it That Way' was John and Edward's song of choice on the night – and the boys nailed it.

John has to bend down as the microphone stand is stuck and Edward looks extremely cute and shy as he sings. 'It was hard getting up in front of everyone in the entire school but we drew on our inner confidence I guess,' Edward recalls. 'Once we got up there it was just so much fun. We didn't really have a dance routine, we just sang.'

The lads' brave performance also came to the attention of their followers on the Internet. On YouTube over 3000 people have commended them on their bravery. One fan wrote: 'They were so young. It's amazing. They had so much courage to get up in front of all those people in a school where they were bullied.'

Another said: 'Aaw, Edward looks so shy here it's fantastic to see how much more confident he's become now! (did anyone else find that little nervous tug to his trouser leg at 0.12 adorable?!) :D. It's obvious that they've both wanted what they have now for a long time and I'm delighted that their dreams are coming true. Their resilience and ambition is truly inspiring!'

In the middle of the song, girls from the school get to their feet and start to clap, cheering for John and Edward: the boys have whipped the teenage girls into a frenzy. John and Edward were fast becoming popular among the female population.

The twins stayed strong and worked even harder on their singing and dancing. 'I think that each time we did a school show, we wanted to do better than the last time,' John says. 'We would look at videos and learn off these moves and routines and stuff.'

In 2007, the twins took to the stage once again to entertain their classmates with a performance of Justin Timberlake's 'Love Stoned'. This time, the lads had transformed themselves from cute, shy singers to dancing and entertaining performers. John and Edward had spent weeks rehearsing and were even granted a team of backing dancers featuring girls from their school.

Again, this video was posted on YouTube. Although much of the crowd can be heard cheering for John and Edward and enjoying themselves, a small group of lads can also be heard laughing and jeering them. The clip has become really popular with Jedward fans. One supporter wrote: 'Question for all the bullies and the people that were laughing, are you now famous all over Europe and are you all millionaires?..... thought not. love you John and? Edward! xxxxx'.

And another said: 'Can't believe those people laughing :o

I seriously hope they are regretting it now they are making money :D It takes a lot of guts to do what they did.'

The twins remember all of their performances in school vividly and loved every minute of them.

The boys also went through all the typical growing-up experiences as teenagers together – including their first shave. Edward says: 'I found razor blades and I cut my whole thumb with one. Then I shaved because that is what I had seen my Dad doing but I cut up my whole face. I didn't want to go to school because I had all of these shave marks and I wasn't able to shave correctly. I was like one of those kids from the movies where they had these marks on the top of their faces. I cut under my chin once and I still have a scar there but I think that it's kind of cool.'

The boys informed their parents that they would prefer to switch schools to study for their Leaving Certificate so it was decided that they would attend a school in Dublin City Centre. And so the boys were enrolled in another fee-paying school famous for yielding terrific exam results. John says, 'We went into this school kind of thinking that we could just be anybody's friend. We just wanted to go in there and for people to accept us as we were. The school was amazing.'

Edward adds, 'On our first day there the girls were starting to fight over us!'

During fifth year, John and Edward did study and found the going tough. The school was completely focussed on the Leaving Certificate Examinations that they would have to take there after two years. Although those around them found themselves under lots of pressure, John and Edward were thriving and always eager to get out to their running classes in the evenings.

'We liked getting the bus into town and there was no Saturday school but as it worked out, we were only there for a year.'

The lads sometimes hear people in the crowd booing them when they perform at larger events, but refuse to let it get to them. John says: 'You have to realise that there's more fans than there are haters. Everyone should just look to the people who are nice and just stick to them.' The twins are determined to only concentrate on the positive and don't allow anyone with negative vibes into their lives.

Even though hundreds of thousands of people ganged up on them on the Internet during the *X Factor*, John and Edward held their heads high. 'It's crazy to think that all of those people were out there hating us during the show,' John shrugs. We just had to realise that these people didn't know us personally and that they had a right to an opinion on us.'

The boys are determined to concentrate on meaningful things and, from day to day, to show people that they care. 'Lots of our fans have had a hard time in school and I feel like we are kind of like an escape for them,' Edward says. 'We make them feel a million dollars and we never treat anyone any different when we meet them. The same people you meet on the way up, you meet them on the way back down and word gets around that you are cool.'

John and Edward decided to audition for *X Factor* slap bang in the middle of their Leaving Certificate cycle. Naturally, their parents were anxious that they should continue their studies. The deal was that they could go and see how they got on at the audition stage but then return to school that September for Sixth Year so that they could begin to study for their final exams. The Leaving Certificate is the Irish equivalent to A-Levels in the UK and is vital to gain entry into colleges.

But John and Edward had very different plans ...

chapter three
run, Jedward, run!

FROM A VERY YOUNG age, John and Edward's family can remember them running around the place as fast as their legs could carry them. The energetic little boys were constantly racing each other as children and developed an interest in running as a hobby.

'We were always healthy and kind of moving around and not spending much time in front of a computer or things like that,' John recalls. 'And then it was like, the faster that you run, the more energy you get. We just, like, got addicted to it and loved every minute. At one point we liked it as much as music – there's like this kind of freedom and you can just run away from anything. We are fast, too.'

The boys aren't exaggerating.

John and Edward had spent some time racing for the Lucan Harriers club where they thrived after moving to

Lucan from Rathangan in Co. Kildare. But they had their eyes on a bigger prize. When they transferred to the school in Dublin City Centre in 2008, they decided that a change was also in order for their running careers. If music was their first love, running was a very close second and John and Edward excelled at the sport.

Eddie Mc Donagh, who used to train them at Dundrum Athletics Club, remembers John and Edward as hard-working young boys with potential to be the best in Ireland.

'Oh there's no doubt about it, when John and Edward came to me, they were going places soon enough,' Eddie says. 'These were two very determined young individuals who had so much energy to burn – they were great runners.'

Ambitious John and Edward contacted Eddie after hearing that he was one of the most sought-after trainers in the country. The boys were even willing to go miles out of their way to attend training every night of the week. Eddie was bowled over by their enthusiasm and it wasn't long before he agreed to train John and Edward. 'They approached me a couple of years ago and I could see from the beginning that they were very, very ambitious,' Eddie remembers.

The trainer had already spotted the speedy blonde-haired twins running with a rival club at a number of events around the country. 'I'd seen them run with another club. Then one day they came to me and said that they would like to train. That's how it started really – I put them to work straight away.'

Dundrum hosts one of the most successful athletic clubs in Ireland and is home to well-known runner David

Gillick. If John and Edward were going to run, they were determined to run for the best. 'I think it says a lot about them that they showed the initiative to come to us and ask us to train them,' Eddie admits. 'They both knew the amount of work that would be required of them to get ahead. Both of them were bursting with energy and just did everything that they were asked from the very beginning.'

With John and Edward, Eddie knew that he was on to a winner straight away. 'I could see that they were very, very good runners from the off. And they were committed. I mean, they were prepared to go all the way from Lucan, into school in the city centre, then come out here to train and then head home again. They both did that five days a week and never missed a session – it shows that they are made of tough stuff and nothing was going to stop them.'

Eddie set out a gruelling schedule of training from Monday to Friday and the boys also continued to run when they were at home at the weekends. 'They were with me for about a year and a half in total,' Eddie says. 'Both of them were training very hard and they wanted to be the best – that was a good start.'

He put the twins through their paces with tough mountain treks and speed-running sessions at Belfield Campus at University College Dublin. 'They were up for it all and worked very hard and within a year I could see a huge improvement. They really had become extremely fast over a relatively short space of time.'

Eddie also remembers the boys as being extremely popular with the other runners in the club. 'They had this kind of infectious energy and people really liked that,' he says. They both got on well with everyone but we thought they just wanted to run. We didn't know that they wanted to get into the entertainment industry at all.'

Eddie first noticed that John and Edward had hidden talents when the club went on a trip to a competition in Cardiff, Wales. 'I remember that they brought a guitar with them and we were kind of surprised at that,' he says. 'We were competing in a team event and we won that event with John and Edward on the team.

'Then, that evening, we were waiting at the train station and they got the guitar out and started singing. I think we were all surprised at that – and they were actually pretty good. Within a few minutes, there was a huge crowd of people around them listening to what they had to sing – it was great!'

Another thing that Eddie remembers about John and Edward's running habits was that they were never too far away from one another on the track. 'I think it was kind of a twin thing, but they used to run together as much as they would run against each other,' he recalls. 'John came first in the Dublin Regional Championships and Edward came second. Then they came third and fourth in an All Ireland competition – as soon as they started to train properly, they were immediately successful.'

Eddie is firmly of the opinion that running provided the optimum energy release for the hyperactive twins. 'You could see that their energy levels were extremely high. They were even hyper while running! They helped each other and were never much further than a foot apart from one another. I had to keep them under control and tell them to pace themselves. They would just bolt out there and have to be ahead of everyone else. They would just run and run all day long.'

After a year of training, the boys were clocking up nearly 50 miles a week running. Eddie and the team at Dundrum had huge hopes for the spiky-haired duo. Eddie was gutted when the twins decided to follow their dreams of making music. 'We were very sorry to lose them, there's no doubt about that,' he says. 'We had the best running team in the country and then when *The X Factor* came along, that was broken. But I do not begrudge them anything at all – we are extremely proud of them and glad that they followed their dreams.'

At weekends, the boys' team-mates at the club used to gather together while they were on the show to watch their former running pals perform.

'I think that a lot of the girls were interested at the beginning,' Eddie chuckles. 'The boys didn't think that it was cool to be supporting them but they soon came around.'

Eddie recently met up with his old protégées and was glad to see that fame has not gone to their heads. He says: 'We met up for about a half an hour at Dundrum Shopping Centre not too long ago and they were asking for everyone at the club straight away. After everything that happened to them in the past year, the first thing that they did was ask about everyone else, which was great to see.'

But Eddie noticed that the usually super-fit boys were looking a bit tired. 'They told me that they had been touring non-stop and hadn't had a chance to go running –

they said that they were missing it. I think that both of them were keen to get back out there for a run because it gave them so much energy. After training so hard for so long, they were really keen to get back out there.'

And their supportive former coach is hoping that, some day, John and Edward will get back to the track at Dundrum. 'I told them that the door is always open for them here,' he says. 'We would welcome them back to the club with open arms. Hopefully they will get back at some stage and run with us. It was a way of life and it was a healthy life. It was how they could use up all that energy. They needed it.

'They were running really good in the end. After a year of training they were doing 10 or 12 mile runs every weekend and then less during the week. They got up to 50 miles a week – they were aiming for something. They have a lot of drive. It didn't come as a surprise to see them do so well. They had something extra, they had something different. I was proud.'

John and Edward had trained tirelessly during their time at Dundrum, often heading out late at night or early in the morning to do extra training. 'We preferred long distance because I think that was a bit more of a challenge,' Edward admits. 'I suppose it was like just running and running and running and seeing how far that you could go before running out of energy.'

Even though they are undoubtedly as close twins as one could meet, John and Edward did experience some rivalry on the running track. John shrugs: 'Well, a race is a race and as much as I would want Edward to do well, I would want to do well too – but we would always want to help each other out. The perfect thing would be if we came in a joint position but that didn't really happen because it's not really possible. Sometimes he would do better and sometimes I would do better and it made it a little bit more of a challenge.'

Even though running is a sport with a great variety of distances, John and Edward were, more often than not, running in the same race. 'We didn't really like to do things on our own,' Edward recalls. 'I mean, even when we were out running, I would look to see where John was. I think it kind of pushed us to do better because, like, we didn't like being behind each other. It was just this thing that we liked to do together – and we would end up, like, running beside each other at the same speed sometimes because we were just alike.'

In December 2008, John came fifth and Edward sixth in the Dublin and District Schools Cross Country League – proving that they always liked to stick together. More often than not, the boys crossed the finishing line pretty near to one another.

'We don't like to just sit around,' John shrugs. 'Like, there's all of this energy there and you want to do something with it and just sitting there isn't going to do anything. Everyone thinks that you would be tired after running like that but we never were.

'We miss it now,' he adds. 'Sometimes when we are on tour we just want to get out of the bus or car and run instead.

'We were always running around the garden at home

when we were young and setting up these races with Kevin, our brother. We ran short races a few times but they were always too short and we just wanted to stay going.

'Mountain running is loads of fun and pretty hard because it's not like flat. We can't even go to a running track now for a shoot or something without wanting to race around it. I don't know what it is.'

In March 2009, the pair came seventh and thirteenth in the Irish Schools Mountain Running Championships in March 2009 – one of their last ever competitive bouts before *X Factor* would take over their lives. Indeed, the boys were really beginning to come into their stride as *X Factor* kicked off for them.

'It wasn't like we decided that it was one or the other because we could always run but just not as much with the show,' Edward remembers. 'Running is just so much fun – I think that we will always do it. It was always kind of cool if we got medals too. But I think we would run anyway, even if there wasn't a race and even if there were no medals.'

Another thing that the twins have to thank running for is their trademark hair. Both John and Edward hated their hair getting into their eyes while running and used to flick it back. Soon after their first try-out for *X Factor*, the twins would learn that their novel look was setting them apart from the crowd and continued to let it grow.

John remembers: 'We used to laugh and push it back and joke that it was going to make us go faster and faster when we were running. We just kind of kept cutting it at the sides and then making it longer on top and it used to blow up in the air when we were running – maybe it did make us faster after all.'

The twins' parents are equally proud of their running feats and display medals throughout their house. 'I think that John and Edward showed great commitment and dedication to their running that will always stand to them in later life,' their mother Susanna says. 'They were committed and would never want to miss training – as soon as school was over they would be getting ready to run and they really excelled.

'It was great for them and they got to travel extensively with it and we often went to support them. They were determined fellows from a very early age, I have to say. And because they were always bouncing around the place with seemingly endless energy levels, running was a fantastic way for them to focus all that energy. It was ideal for them, really, and they still love it to this very day. I think that both John and Edward will always run – they have a passion for it.'

The twins themselves admit that running was a place where they could go to escape all of the pressures of the world. John says: 'I remember that running was always like my safe place where I would go to. It was one of the places that you knew that you had your friends and that they could come running with you.'

As with many things that John and Edward did, it was their granddad Kevin who encouraged them to take up running in the first place. Loving Kevin thought that it would be a great way for the energetic twosome to put their high energy levels to good use. It was Kevin who took the twins to their first-ever running club in Lucan and John and Edward admit that they were hooked from the very first day.

Edward recalls his granddad talking to them about taking up the sport and thinking that they would love it. 'As usual, our granddad was right,' Edward says. 'He thought that we could do it and told us that we could be really good at it and then we were. Basically, the running track was across our road and it was a really rainy night and we didn't know if we were going to go over or not.'

But the boys' practice with games of Cops and Robbers had meant that they were already super-fast when they began to train at 12 years of age. 'With our first club, we thought we were good,' John says. 'But then when we moved to Dundrum, we realised that we weren't that good and we were going to have to get a whole lot better.'

Now that their schedule involves them being on the road most of the time, John and Edward really miss taking out their running shoes and heading off into the distance. 'Cross country was our favourite,' John says. 'And everyone in the club was really cool and we felt like we belonged there. Like, everyone was so passionate about running and wanted everyone to do their very best. I think me and Edward could feel that there and just pushed ourselves to get better and better. We were really good in the end, and I think that we could be really good again if we went back to all of the training that we used to do. Maybe we could go to the Olympics in 2016 – we will still be young then and able to do it and we could be like the first pop stars to win gold medals.'

Both John and Edward reckon that if they had not become involved in *X Factor*, they could have gone on to great things in athletics. If they hadn't pursued their dreams of superstardom, they might now be in training for the Olympics.

John shrugs: 'I think that we could have maybe made it to the Olympics if we tried hard enough. Like, running was our passion and we would run all day long if we got the chance. And the thing is, that when we left running, we were actually just getting really really good at it. It was like we ran with one another instead of against one another and got ourselves through all of the races. And when we started getting medals and stuff, it all began to really pay off. I reckon we would have been great if we had stayed running, but we didn't.'

But one thing that they are both keen to get across to young fans is the importance of exercise. The twins, who live on a diet of healthy sushi, chicken, all types of fruit and vegetables, water, juices and cereal, are all about clean living and fresh air.

Edward feels that young children need to become involved in sport from a very early age and to stick to it. 'I mean, think about it, OK? It's a way to meet friends, get exercise and just feel really good about yourself,' he says. 'If you sit around all day watching TV and playing games inside you are not going to feel very good and you won't have much energy. You don't see as many kids out all over the place as when we were younger and that's kind of sad. Maybe the whole "stranger danger" thing has everyone scared but kids should just get outside into their back gardens or wherever and just play – it's that easy.'

John and Edward carry their active and healthy lifestyle through everything, from their eating patterns to how much exercise they get. Years of healthy eating has made them ideal candidates for life on the road and they always pay close attention to nutrition and what goes into their bodies.

John admits: 'Right now, we just eat loads of sushi and tuna fish. We often go to Marks & Spencer and just get loads of it.'

The twins are also constantly eating fruit and vegetables. 'It's not like it's a conscious thing, it's just that healthy things are things we like the most,' Edward shrugs. 'And we don't drink tea or coffee or fizzy drinks or anything like that – we just have water. I think that when we used to be training, we ate healthy foods and now we are just used to all of that.'

When they go home to Lucan, their mother Susanna prepares their favourite meals, but they stay away from fast food restaurants while on the road. Everyone thinks that we are vegetarians, but we are not. We love steamed chicken, fish and steamed vegetables and that's what we would eat if we were at home.'

John and Edward are glad that their hectic touring schedule means that they get lots of exercise running around on-stage. Not ones just to sit down and do nothing, both John and Edward say that they need to be active each and every day and will rarely be found just sat in a corner doing nothing.

Edward says: 'I think that's why we put so much energy into our performances – because we used to put it all into our running. We love doing handstands and flips and jumping all around the place – we just don't really know how to just sit down and do nothing. John and I are all about getting things done and the more you run around, the more energy you have. No-one wants to go to a concert and just see two people standing there – it's like, come on and get a move on and entertain us! All of the best entertainers go a bit crazy on stage and we try to never stop moving.'

The twins try to get back to their old running club as often as possible and hope that they will always able to keep up the sport – even if it's just as a hobby. 'When we see people running in the street we are always talking about the way they are running, if they are going too slow or too fast,' John says. 'It's like we want to be out there running instead of them and we are jealous because we are sitting in traffic or something. We didn't really like running on the track – getting out and doing cross country was what we really loved.

'I think that we will always be running one way or another and it's a sport that we would never want to leave behind. I don't think that we will look back with any regrets, though, because now we are living the dream, really, and we are happy with how things worked out.

'You can't have everything, but one day we will be back on the track and running as a team again. We haven't gone away forever!'

Chapter Four

red carpet fever

WHEN THE BOYS started to attend school in Dublin city, they began to get a taste for the limelight. Both John and Edward were tired of sitting around and dreaming about being famous – they wanted to make their dreams come true. The boys set about making their own online MySpace page and finding out where film premières and other posh events were taking place around town so that they could head along.

When they weren't at school or running training, it was time for John and Edward to get their glad rags on and try to get noticed. John remembers: 'We would walk down the street in Dublin and there would be these events happening – it wasn't really like we were out looking for them all of the time but sometimes we would just go to see what was happening and who we could meet.'

The boys' interest in fashion was also there from an early age. When John and Edward hit their teens, they started to

47

develop their own unique sense of style. And once they started hitting top events in town, they wanted to get noticed but were short on cash. 'I remember we used to go into vintage shops and pick out these really cool jackets and ties and just end up looking amazing,' Edward grins. 'We could go into those shops and just pick up things that someone else didn't want and make it work. We would go to premières and stuff and people thought that we were famous then. We were basically in training camp, OK? That was like when we were out learning the trade and finding out how it all worked.'

While John and Edward attended class during the day, their dreams of showbiz domination were never too far from their minds. The twins used to practise their autograph on their text books and laugh as they remember one student who told them that they would never achieve fame. 'Those kinds of things just made us more determined,' John says. 'I remember I started practising my autograph when I was eight years old because I knew that I was going to need a good one for when I got older – we knew what we were doing.'

The boys even managed to meet The Pussycat Dolls at one awards ceremony in Dublin and grabbed the babes' attention. But both are keen to add that they 'weren't these losers who were following them around.' Edward reveals: 'We weren't stalking people, we just wanted to see what it was like to be around that kind of thing. Loads of people would push us to the side and think that they were famous and we were no-one. People were so rude and would turn their faces away from you on the street.'

But the pair persisted and soon grabbed the attention of local photographers in Dublin who were working in showbusiness. Photographer Gareth from online site Showbiz.ie can remember John and Edward turning up at events around the city in the early days. 'I thought that they were great kids and they used to hang around and try to get pictures with the stars. It's amazing to look at them in action now and to think that just a couple of years ago, they were on the other side of the barrier. I knew them from the very early days, and they don't forget you either. They are still lovely, lovely lads.'

Gareth knew that the boys were serious about the business when he kept meeting them at events. 'They seemed very interested in everything that the stars were doing and would ask them questions,' he said. 'They weren't just there to meet them – they seemed to be there so that they could find out more about the industry.'

Indeed, John and Edward's quest for knowledge about the industry developed into a love of reading books about their favourite celebrities. They own shelf-loads of biographies and autobiographies of stars like Britney Spears, The Jonas Brothers and Miley Cyrus. 'We wanted to see how they all got to where they are,' Edward says. 'They had all been on a journey and hadn't all been, like, pop stars since they were young so we love reading all about them.'

The twins also devoured hours of documentaries and life stories of their favourite celebrities on satellite TV channels. It is now a lifetime ambition of theirs to have their story told on the E! Channel in the USA. 'All of the big names have their True Hollywood stories,' John says.

'We should have one too some day. Like, there's so much stuff that we have managed to fit into a year – so imagine how much more we are going to do in the next couple of years! We love Joan Rivers and Ellen and people like that and would just love to get on their shows some day. America kind of feels like home to us and we always loved American TV and American stars.'

As the lads became more and more focussed on becoming famous, their parents wondered if they were making the right choice. But John and Edward told them to have faith, and that their dreams would come true. 'It was never a Plan B for us – it was always Plan A,' John shrugs. 'It was the main aim; from a young age we just wanted to perform and entertain people and to travel all over the world.'

Edward adds: 'I think that when you have this vision of something, then you can make it happen.' But the lads' dreams weren't without a reality check from their parents, who naturally were keen for them to concentrate on their studies.

As the months passed by, both John and Edward became more and more focussed on achieving their dreams. 'We would make ourselves look amazing, leave the house and go and see what would happen,' recalls John.

Even when they would just make a trip to their local shopping centre at Liffey Valley, long before they became famous, the boys attracted attention from onlookers. Model agent Fiona Roche from Rogue Model Management in Dublin says that this comes as no surprise: 'When you take away the Jedward persona and the X

Factor and everything else here, what you have are two stunning-looking guys. The fact that they are identical, tall and just so full of personality would have made it impossible not to notice John and Edward. Even when you see them now, you can't but look at the boys – they are perfect model material and even if they were not on TV, I would imagine that they would always have girls flocking to them.'

When they weren't out getting attention at premières and shopping centres, John and Edward would spend time in their bedroom in Lucan practising their singing and learning different dance moves from their music videos. They are convinced that the fact that they came from a small place meant that they were destined for greater things. 'Think about it,' John says. 'Britney Spears came from Louisiana and no-one even knew where that was before she was famous. She made her way out there and did it and it's the same thing with me and Edward. We are, like, from Lucan and we do our thing. No-one ever thought that we would get famous – but we did.'

John and Edward even took model-style pictures of themselves and set up online pages where people could learn all about them. Years before *The X Factor* even happened, the twins made a video saying: 'John and Edward, coming soon' and posted it on their site. They also superimposed pictures of themselves on red carpets! The boys were so dedicated in their quest for fame that they even got pictures of crowds and made it look like they were at John and Edward concerts. 'I have these videos on one of my old computers and my mom was like, "You have a great imagination", but it did all happen in the end,' Edward says. 'It was like this whole slide show that we had made and it all came true.'

The boys never lost their optimism or determination to succeed and they kept it with them all throughout their years in school. 'I think it's a really, really cool thing to realise that, like, Edward is the same age as me and everything that he has experienced, I have experienced too,' John says. 'We share the exact same birthday. We used to love Mary-Kate and Ashley [Olsen] – we were always influenced by watching US TV and that whole vibe.'

Even their choice of television programmes was determined by the kind of lifestyle that they wanted. John and Edward loved to catch Disney programmes and shows featuring the world's most famous twins, Mary-Kate and Ashley Olsen. But, unusually, neither John nor Edward ever pestered their mother Susanna to send them to drama school. Both were determined that, if they were going to make it, they were going to do it on their own. They also feared that they would lose what it was that made them unique if they had to immerse themselves in a drama school environment. 'I mean, we wanted to make things happen and we just went out there and did that.'

The boys liken themselves to pop queen Lady Gaga who went out and got herself noticed. 'She just got out there and was different from everyone else and that's why she is so amazing,' Edward says. 'You have to be different and stand out from the crowd and that's how we got noticed in the end. People who just go out and act the same as everyone else will never get noticed.'

The boys made tapes of themselves performing and gathered lots of information from talent shows and admit that they were never shy about telling their friends that they wanted to be pop stars. Even though it might be seen by many as a cocky attitude to have, John and Edward had enough belief in themselves just to shrug off people's looks of disbelief when they told them of their dreams. 'Other people dream big but never tell anyone about it and never put it into a reality,' John says. 'We would always dream big and let everyone know. That way, you just had to go out there and make things happen. Otherwise you would just end up looking stupid.'

Although the boys' parents understandably had reservations about letting them become pop stars, they could constantly rely on their granddad Kevin for words of encouragement. Kevin had always told the twins that they should shoot for the stars and that they could do anything that they put their mind to. He had often watched John and Edward perform dancing and singing sequences that they had made up in their bedroom. 'At first, our teddies were our audience, but then our granddad was like our live audience,' Edward says. 'He always enjoyed watching us perform and told us that if we didn't go for things, then they weren't just going to happen. He was the same when it came to running and just wanted us to be the best we could be at everything.'

The twins focussed on fashion as well as performing and wanted to be known as much for their sense of style as for their performances. They knew that to stand out from the crowd, they would have to look different from everyone else. This would lead to the development of 2009's most sought-after hairstyle – The Jedward. 'We didn't always have our hair the way that it is now – the whole style thing just kind of came around,' John says. 'It used to be a lot shorter and darker and then when we went to the UK people were talking about our hair sticking up and we just decided then that it should be bigger and better. It just stayed growing, but it wasn't a big plan. It's like we made something cool without even trying.'

With clothes, John and Edward shunned the popular tracksuit and hoodie approach and always wanted to look smart. They raided relatives' wardrobes and were constantly on the lookout for skinny ties and jackets – two staples that would soon become part of their signature look. 'I think that me and John were always looking out for things, fashion-wise,' Edward says. 'Just things that would make us stand out from the crowd. We were always into fashion from when we were really young and had a say in what we wanted to wear.'

As well as film premières, John and Edward sought out signings that bands were doing at record stores in Dublin and made it their mission to go there and meet artists. They were regulars at many HMV signings in Dublin, where they would later go on to create pandemonium with their own launches.

Irish singer Mundy can recall meeting the twins at one of his own launches in Dublin long before they became famous. He revealed in an interview earlier this year that he could remember them asking to have a picture taken with him at his album launch. 'I can remember the two of them asking to have their picture taken with me,' he said. 'I thought it was kind of strange they had gone to the bother of painting their faces like mine but they seemed real fans and knew all my songs. They weren't half bad singers either. I had no idea I was face to face with what was to become the Jedward phenomenon.'

The twins were just 17 at the time, but were keen to get as much advice as possible about how everything worked in the industry. Mundy remembered them both picking his brain about his career. He said, 'They asked me for advice on how to break into the pop business. They seemed so confident and sure it was going to happen for them. At the time I thought, bless – then six months later there they were on *X Factor*! I was sitting there at home going, "It's those twins. They've done it."'

John and Edward's love of music and interest in the industry soon got them noticed on the scene in Dublin. In May 2009 they went along to the Academy in Dublin for a Battle of The Bands competition called Blastbeat. The twins had no money to get in and Blastbeat founder Robert Stephenson said he would let them in for free if they would help him to judge the competition. John and Edward agreed and joined the panel of judges to give their opinion on who should win. In the end, the band that John and Edward had chosen – Downhill – went on to win the entire competition after the lads backed them.

Irish comedian PJ Gallagher can also remember meeting John and Edward a couple of years ago while he was filming a show in Dublin city centre. Speaking on Brendan O'Connor's chat show (on which the twins also appeared) the comedian said: 'We were filming in George's Arcade and they were like, "Can we be in it? It's really cool, let's be in it!' And we were like, "No, we're working, we're busy." A couple of months later I saw "Ghostbusters" and was, like, shite!'

He added: 'We were just like, "Go away there, lads," so that we could get on with filming and the next thing you knew they were all over the place! It took some guts to come up and say that – they were definitely determined, so fair play. It's great to see them doing so well now.'

Not content with going around town and trying to get noticed, John and Edward also wrote to TV shows in Ireland and the UK, telling them about their talents. As part of their 'you have to make things happen' mentality, the pair were relentless in their quest to get noticed. 'Nothing is going to happen if you just sit around and do nothing,' John shrugs. 'We went to all of these things and talked to people because we wanted to know how it all worked. We were on a learning curve and beginning our training and wanted to get advice from as many people as possible.' The twins wrote to RTE, BBC and even to world-famous TV host Ellen De Generes to tell her about themselves. 'All it takes is one break and then you could make it,' Edward shrugs. 'It really was what we wanted.'

Remarkably, their online fan base began to grow – even though they had never actually performed on TV and nobody really knew who they were. Their quirky posts, good looks and talk of the music industry grabbed the attention of girls on the Internet so John and Edward had an online fan base even before they appeared on *X Factor*.

They also added people in the industry as their friends in a bid to get noticed.

Before auditioning for *X Factor*, John and Edward were already fully aware of the people who worked in the background of the show such as choreographer Brian Friedman. And each day, the boys would day dream about the time that they would finally make it. 'People might read this and think it was sad that we were out there doing all of those things, but so what?' John says. 'As far as I am concerned, if you really want something to happen, you have to go and get it. It's not as if by magic you are going to become well known. If we never went for that first audition on the show, we wouldn't be here now. One decision can change your life forever.'

But even if *The X Factor* hadn't worked out, John and Edward would have still been determined to turn their dreams into a reality. They both say that if they hadn't made it through, they would have kept on trying. 'We were only 17 so we weren't going to give up on our dreams, no matter what happened with *The X Factor*,' Edward says. 'I think that we would just have found another way. Or gone away and practised and come back again, or just camped outside of Louis' office until he noticed us. It wouldn't have been the end.'

John added: 'We went to see Boyz II Men in a venue in Dublin when we were younger and that was really cool and they gave us loads and loads of advice. They have been around for ages and have inspired, like, loads of other boy bands. It was like our first celebrity group to meet.'

Publisher Michael O'Doherty, who owns a number of

glossy magazines in Ireland, also remembers being startled at seeing John and Edward on *The X Factor*. He recalls thinking that they were familiar, but wasn't quite sure why. 'Then it came to me that they had been at lots of launches and red-carpet events that we had. I also remember them coming up to a stand for *Kiss* magazine at one event, and asking if they could have their picture in the mag. They stood out for obvious reasons, and just a year later we would be phoning them up and trying to get interviews – their rise has been phenomenal.' Michael would later find himself sitting backstage in the dressing room of Louis Walsh at *The X Factor*, meeting the twins once again.

As with most of the people they meet in the industry, John and Edward remembered who Michael was and, in particular, his distinctive orange Lamborghini car. Ironically, Michael then had to ask John and Edward to have a photo taken with him so that he could show it to the girls back at the office. 'How the tables have turned,' he smiled while posing with the boys. 'I am never going to live this down!'

Earlier this year the twins featured on the cover of Michael's *VIP* magazine, with a glossy photo shoot included inside. And they could hardly believe how far they had come. 'It's really cool being on the front of magazines in the UK and stuff but in Ireland, that's when it's really special,' John says. 'I mean, we grew up with all of those magazines and looked at the celebs in there and sometimes got our pictures in the social pages and things. So to walk into a shop and see yourself on the cover and know that they were in shops all over the country was really, really cool.'

Manager Louis Walsh admits that the boys' keen interest in how the industry worked before they were famous proved to him that they were genuine and serious about becoming pop stars. 'I don't want to work with people who are just out to do something as a bit of a laugh,' Louis says. 'If you want to get somewhere and you want to succeed, then you have to show that you have an interest. The boys wanted to be pop stars and from the very minute that I saw them, I knew that they could be. You either have that special something or you don't and I thought that they had it in spades. When I heard that some people already knew of them around Dublin, I thought that was good – it meant that they had an interest and weren't doing it just for fun. You have to want it more than anything else in the world and I think that John and Edward really did want it, since they were young teenagers.'

And Louis says that another thing that sets John and Edward apart from the thousands of other people who want to be famous is their memory. No-one can match John and Edward when it comes to meeting people, remembering them and just having winning personalities. 'People who meet John and Edward don't forget them, and John and Edward don't forget the people that they meet,' he says. 'They are nice to everybody, from the people on the street to the people in the record company – and that's why they have so many fans. Everyone wants to work with them because they are just so hard-working and genuinely nice. John and Edward make the people that they meet smile and they make them feel special – that is their secret and that is what sets them apart from a lot of people. Their attitude is 100 per cent positive all of the time and that is why they are where they are now.'

The X Factor was John and Edward's first ever appearance on television. Even though Susanna had been asked about getting them into modelling since they were babies, she chose to keep them grounded and let them have ordinary childhoods. As a result, although the twins are confident, they are not vain or obsessed with their looks. 'Looks are not everything,' Edward says. 'It's not as if we look in the mirror and think that we are gorgeous. 'We like to dress good and do our hair and stand out a little but that doesn't mean that we are vain. We have spotty days and days when we don't feel good, just like everyone.'

And even though they have always received attention from girls, the twins were never going to let romance get in their way of superstardom. 'You have all of your life for that,' John muses. 'We wanted a career and, now we have one, we want to concentrate on that. But the right girl hasn't come along, anyway – maybe things will change if she does.'

And the girls who may finally distract them from their gruelling schedule will have to be very special. 'We don't go for girls who wear loads of make-up and try to look really, really old,' John insists. 'That isn't our type of thing.'

Edward adds: 'We like a girly girl who actually is a girl. Loads of girls used to ask us out and wanted to kiss us and everything. We were never desperate, OK? We wanted to find the right girls.' John feels that there are so many girls that the twins meet but they find it hard to pick just one person. 'It's kind of like, why would you be with just one girl? She would have to be really special.'

But, for now, the duo are content to focus on their music and the journey that they have taken in the past 12 months. 'Just a couple of years ago, this was all a dream,' John says. 'We used to watch the clock in school and then run down to launches and things and try to get noticed. We loved the flashing of cameras, meeting celebs and getting autographs from people there. Now that we are on, like, the other side of the ropes, we aren't going to forget the other people. We were over there with our dreams just a while ago – we made it all happen and so can everyone else if they want to.'

Edward adds: 'You have to remember everyone on the way up and we still meet photographers and people who remember when we were just dressed up going around Dublin. I don't think that you will ever see us running away from our fans and covering our faces. We are, like, so lucky to be where we are and all we ever do is want to say "hi" to our fans and talk to them. They have always stood beside us and they are our friends. We ask their opinion on everything and I think too many people forget how they got somewhere in the first place. We won't forget anything like that and everyone says that this won't last forever, but me and John are planning on making it last for as long as we can.'

chapter five

WHEN aLL aroUND THEM WOULD CHanGE

AFTER WATCHING THE previous year's *X Factor*, the boys
had decided that they would like to audition in 2009.
Having seen the hopefuls go through to the live finals and
get the thumbs-up from judges Simon Cowell, Dannii
Minogue, Louis Walsh and Cheryl Cole, they were sure they
had what it took to get through.

While sitting at home in 2008, the twins had been
watching the show with their beloved grandfather Kevin
when he suggested that they should audition. Every single
year, the boys had tuned into the show and watched with
their whole family on Saturday nights.

'Our granddad told us every year that we should go for
it and then we just decided that we would,' says John. 'Our
granddad was basically the main person that said, "You
could do that," – and we did do it.'

The twins went on the Internet to fill out their application forms online and waited to hear back from the show's producers. They soon got the call and had to organise a flight over to the UK for the first round of auditions in the summer of 2009. Parents John and Susannah arranged their flights and agreed to travel over to the UK so that the boys could audition.

And from day one, John and Edward had a plan – they were going to get noticed. Having studied the movements of celebrities and watched hours of the show, they knew that wallflowers and shrinking violets would never get any attention: John and Edward were going to make themselves known.

John recalls their very first audition when they took to the queue with thousands upon thousands of other hopefuls. The twins woke up early in the morning and had to head for the tube station to make their way to the auditions. Always early risers, John and Edward woke their father before 5am to secure their place in the queue. In fact, they were there so early that they found themselves near the very top – a strategy they had already planned out at home.

'Once we were there we stood out from everyone else, and started singing and dancing and getting noticed by the cameras because otherwise what's the point in going?' asks John. 'The camera crew all came over to us: they had scouted us, basically. There was loads of people around us who did seem really, really good but we just wanted to stand out.'

And stand out they certainly did. When the auditionees

were told to stand up, John and Edward sat down – and when they were told to sit down, the boys stood up. 'I think that you have to be confident or else you are not going to get anywhere on shows like that,' John admits.

Following this, the boys got the thumbs-up and even managed to gather some fans in the queues on their first day in London. 'When we went to the first audition, we had to sing in front of producers and then they told us to go along to Glasgow to sing in front of the judges,' Edward adds. 'We came back to Ireland and for a couple of weeks rehearsed some songs in our bedroom. The thing about it is, you have to have more than one song ready in case Simon or someone else doesn't like the one you picked, so you have to be ready.'

John and Edward were determined to get mentally ready for the next phase and to wow the judges, so the boys picked a couple of their favourite Backstreet Boys' songs. While in the middle of preparing for their audition in front of the judges, the twins found out that particular year's trials would be in front of a live audience for the first time ever. Previously, all hopefuls had sung in front of just the judges in a private room, but Simon Cowell decided that a shake-up was needed in 2009 and decided to see how the contestants would perform in front of a live audience of up to 5,000 people. *The X Factor* would now follow the format of shows such as *Britain's Got Talent*, where hopefuls were often booed and heckled by the crowds if they didn't like their auditions.

But Edward reckoned that going in front of a live audience could work to their advantage: 'I think we thought that we could just go out there and entertain the audience from the start and if they liked us, then the judges would hear them cheer and like us. So we kind of pretended that it was a little mini John and Edward concert. We weren't really nervous when we saw the judges – we had weeks to get ready and I don't know, we were just ready and wanted to go for it. We were tired of waiting.'

When the boys first went in to audition, they saw the judges backstage before they went out to perform. For once in their lives, the pair was stuck for words and didn't know what to say. Edward recalls: 'I remember thinking that they all looked way better in real life. Dannii Minogue looked really good in comparison to on TV. Louis is the ultimate legend and he had a big welcome for us. All of the other acts were star-struck by their mentors but we never got like that with Louis. We always knew exactly what to say to him and we were never nervous.'

John and Edward are grateful to Louis for the advice he gave them and say that he was always on the other end of the phone if they ever needed someone to talk to. From the outset, they felt that Louis could relate to them better than the other judges because he too was Irish. Although they never told anyone else, secretly they had been hoping that Walsh would be the one to get the groups category after the boot-camp stages of the show.

'We were the first contestants to ever go on *Sky News* because Louis got us on *Sky News*,' Edward says. 'He used to sneak us out of the show and lead us over to the cameras across the road to talk to *Sky News*. All of the other competitors would have been inside watching TV and wondering how the hell we got to get on the news and campaign for votes – all of that was down to Louis Walsh.'

The twins say that one of their manager's primary pieces of advice to them was 'always break the rules'. And they are grateful that he himself always broke the rules for them while the show was on. 'He wasn't supposed to sneak us out but he didn't care,' John grins. 'Louis always tells us to never follow the rules and always break out and be different: but we don't attention seek, things just work out well for us.'

Back to the first audition with the judges and John and Edward came before Simon, Dannii, Cheryl and Louis wearing sharp navy blazers, school ties and their soon-to-be trademark boot runners. Given this was the first year that Cowell had decided to audition hopefuls in front of a live audience, the twins were determined to make an entrance – and, as usual, they did.

Both John and Edward walked out confidently in front of the 5,000-strong audience and the four very intimidating judges. Immediately they asked the crowd if they were 'ready to party'. If ever a lesson was needed in how to make an entrance, this was it. From the off, the boys had the attention of every single person in the theatre.

And, as if he can already see a vision for the future, Louis is shown smiling broadly and asking the twins who they are.

Edward: 'We're twins. I'm Edward.'
John: 'And I'm John, and we're 17 and we're from Dublin.'

Witty Cheryl was quick to remark: 'It's a yes from Louis,' while Simon asked them why they were speaking in American accents. 'Look guys, you are from Ireland: be Irish, don't talk in an American accent,' he told them. Just two minutes after arriving on-stage and the twins were already being subjected to the wrath of Cowell, the show's mastermind.

John drew more laughter from the crowd and the judges when Cheryl asked them where they saw themselves in 15 years' time and he said: 'Well, I see myself getting older.' Louis then asked the boys why they wanted to become pop stars and they told him that they had travelled to see 'all the ladies', including Cheryl and Dannii.

After five minutes' banter Simon ordered them to 'just sing the song' and John and Edward launched into the Backstreet Boys' hit 'As Long As You Love Me'. The audience – and Louis – loved the performance but Simon dubbed it 'not very good and incredibly annoying.'

'Two of the most irritating people we have had out here in a long, long time,' he declared, while Cheryl added: 'There is something intriguing about you, but I just don't know if it's in a good way.'

But it seemed that the pair, with their confident attitude and great looks, had already won over judge Louis. 'You really do look like pop stars, you know?' he told them. 'I think you have got something, I do think you can be worked on, yeah.'

Meanwhile, Aussie judge Dannii Minogue described them as 'absolutely the cockiest couple of singers I've ever come across that don't have a record deal yet, but I like you, guys.'

Finally, the moment of truth arrived and the fate of John and Edward's singing career lay in the hands of the four judges. Simon was first out of the traps and gave a clear and concise no, but the gods were shining on the boys as Dannii, Cheryl and Louis gave them definite thumbs-up. And so the wait had been worth it – John and Edward had won over most of the judges and were on their way to *X Factor* boot camp! The thrilled pair ran backstage and immediately got on the phone to tell the rest of their family.

'I think for a minute we were a bit worried because Simon was saying that we had American accents, and were annoying and all this,' John recalls. 'But I was just up there, thinking: wow, Simon Cowell is talking to me and Edward! Louis was smiling all of the time and so was Cheryl, and we were glad that we made them laugh. It was a long day and you only get, like, two minutes on that stage so anything could happen, but we got through.'

John and Edward then returned to Dublin holding the biggest secret of their lives. The show's producers issued a stern warning that they were not to tell anyone that they had auditioned or were through to boot camp and they would be in touch.

At the time, Edward likened those weeks of secrecy to 'some sort of secret society'.

'We would just be in our room practising for boot camp and dying to tell everyone but we couldn't tell anyone because then that would ruin the show.'

For a number of weeks the boys continued to enjoy their summer holidays and prepared for boot camp – a couple of days that could change their lives forever. 'We knew that loads of people don't make it past boot camp and then you never see them again, so we knew there was lots of work to be done,' says John. 'No one in Ireland had a clue, though, and that was kind of fun. We just wanted to get in front of the judges again and see what they had to say about us.

'We practised all of the time at home before going back over to London – we knew that not many people get second chances on the show so if you get through the first time, you have to make it happen then or it could just all be over.'

On 31 July 2009, the *Irish Sun* broke the news that a pair of Irish twins had made it through to the second round of *X Factor*. The boys' names hit the showbiz section for the first time that day – and would rarely be out of the pages again. Reports from the *X Factor* camp were that John and Edward had already divided the judges on whether or not they were talented enough.

One insider revealed: 'The Grimes made an impression from day one. They are really funny guys who are mad about their music and determined to make it. The girls already love them – even if they can be overconfident.'

The story of the twins' success was soon being reported in news outlets all over Ireland as journalists scrambled to gather as much information as possible on them. At this point, it turned out that John and Edward's aspirations for stardom were already evident via their MySpace website. The ambitious pair were already friends with several leading players in the industry including dance instructor Brian Friedman, Simon Cowell's right-hand woman Sinitta and members of the Backstreet Boys. Already pictures of the twins in pop-star poses had been posted as they urged their 'fans' to support them, even though few people at the time knew who they were.

The twins also posted a range of pictures of themselves at showbiz events all around Dublin, where they were dressed to impress. It was obvious that John and Edward had been hungry for a showbiz career for some time before *X Factor*.

On 30 July, the boys began the gruelling boot-camp stages of the show with over 100 other competitors and had just days to win their place on the show. And it wasn't going to be an easy ride: hopefuls found themselves woken up at the crack of dawn after singing late into the night.

At one point, John and Edward were even split up and put into different groups to see how they gelled with other hopefuls. But the duo was determined and so the fight was on and they would do whatever they had to do to survive. At boot camp, the boys were put through their paces and had to endure days of waiting to learn if they were going to make it through to the group finals.

Meanwhile, word of their involvement in *X Factor* had spread back home and journalists were already beginning to knock on the door of their parents' home in Lucan. But the twins had to keep everything top secret and barely told their close family and group of friends what was going on.

On their final audition in front of the judges, Jedward – who were still just known as The Grimes Twins – wowed judges with an a capella version of Michael Jackson's 'You Are Not Alone'.

'I think that was the first time that we realised they really could sing,' Louis admits. 'I mean, they had this really unusual look and this novelty factor because they were twins, but despite what everyone thinks they needed to be able to hold a note.

'It wouldn't be fair not to put other people through and let groups that clearly can't sing in with a shot of getting to the finals. They had to show us that they could sing and, thankfully, on that day they managed to do just that.'

The boys were paired up with girl group Misfits and solo hopeful Sian Paley to sing in front of the judges. Presenter Dermot O'Leary caught up with them on the second day of boot camp and told them that there had been 'very mixed feedback' about their performances.

Despite Simon dubbing them 'two of the most irritating people we've had out here in a long, long time', John and Edward weren't fazed and were determined to win him over. Edward admitted: 'We have taken the judges' comments on board and got our harmonies – we might tone it down a bit. No, we won't – it's just an audition.'

The boys vowed to give it their all and even though they were in a group scenario, they were determined to showcase themselves. When the three acts took to the stage, Edward went it alone, causing Louis to remark: 'Where's the other one?' After Edward enquired, 'Where is my twin?', John made his entrance via somersaults from one side of the stage.

Simon Cowell gave his trademark scowl as Dannii bit her pen and Cheryl was filmed shaking her head and looking none too happy – it seemed as though John and Edward were in trouble.

The twins had spent hours working on 'Apologise' with their fellow group members and started off the song together. As they danced across the stage, Louis giggled and Simon once again shook his head in dismay. The audition wasn't helped when the boys seemed to forget their words.

When the song was over, Simon told solo hopeful Sian: 'Quite simply, you became invisible.' She then asked to say something and told the judges that Jedward had sung over her parts of the song. A defiant John and Edward shrugged and muttered, 'No, we didn't' and then said that they had mixed up some of the words and decided to sing another bit of the song.

Their cheeky move meant it was make or break for them on *The X Factor*. Either the judges would see it as unfair and a form of cheating or admire them for fighting their corner. In an exercise that was supposed to be about teamwork with other groups, John and Edward had managed to make it all about them: the gloves were off and they would take no prisoners.

'When we mixed up some of the words we got a real fright and kind of thought, oh no, we have blown everything and they are going to send us home,' Edward recalls. 'So we both just kind of kept singing so that they could keep hearing us and maybe forget that we had missed some of our part. I think most people would have done the same.'

The boys' move was to prove vital to their success – if Simon liked their ruthless and ambitious approach to the audition, they would be laughing. Unsurprisingly, he admitted that he admired the fact that John and Edward had forgotten about working as a team and had showcased themselves instead. And Louis Walsh was in agreement, saying: 'I think the boys have got potential, Simon. I think that kids are going to like these guys. I think they have got potential.'

Even though Cowell had liked their approach, he wasn't convinced about the twins' singing ability and was overheard telling Louis that he thought they were 'two brats', to which Louis replied: 'No Simon, they are innocent children.' Cowell added: 'They are vile little creatures who would step on their mother's head to have a hit.'

And so John and Edward and the Misfits both sailed through the round, while angry solo singer Sian was forced to go home. The boys were through to Judges' Houses and fame and superstardom was finally within their grasp!

Immediately, the thrilled youngsters rang their grandparents to tell them the good news. They were then instructed to pack their bags and head to the airport on a specific date in August, when they would meet the mentor of the groups. Once again, the twins returned to their house in Lucan bursting with excitement and holding a big secret.

By now, the media was well on the trail of their story and journalists had begun knocking on the door and calling at neighbours to see what information they could glean about the blue-eyed blond boys who were taking the show by storm. John and Edward remember their granddad telling them that journalists were calling round to his house and some had even contacted their family in Kildare and Limerick to see what they could find out.

'That was hard because we couldn't really talk to anyone and all we wanted to do was run around and tell everybody,' John admits. 'For weeks, we knew we were going to boot camp but had to just carry on as if everything was normal. It was worth it in the end, though.'

While neither of them had any idea who would be in charge of the groups, both John and Edward wanted Louis Walsh to mentor them. The twins knew that Louis had liked them more than any of the other judges at boot camp and they understood that their chances of success would be heightened if pop svengali Walsh was in charge of the groups: if Louis was their mentor, they might get through to the live finals. Little did they know that they had another battle ahead in the form of Boyzone star, Ronan Keating.

The boys were whisked off to a villa in Italy with the other finalists in the group category in August 2009. Upon hearing Italy was the destination of choice, their hearts sank – in the past Louis had always taken his finalists somewhere in Ireland for the Judges' Houses section of the show. But John, Edward and the other hopefuls were in for a surprise: Louis had decided that a change was as good as a rest and had rented a luxury villa on Lake Como to make his final selections.

John and Edward were over the moon to learn that Louis was in fact mentoring the groups and got to work on their all-important audition the minute they arrived in Italy. John says: 'We knew that it was now or never and this could be the last-ever time that we were going to be singing on the show. We were so excited to get to Italy but had to just concentrate on our performance – we knew it was going to be hard, but it was harder than we thought.'

The ambitious twins were filmed practising their dance moves by the villa's pool and spoke of their aspirations to 'have a hit album and go out with Britney Spears.' Edward even came out with the spooky premonition: 'John and Edward have big hair, now I think that everyone is going to have big hair.'

In the sweltering heat, the boys walked up the steps of the villa to face Louis and his helper, Boyzone star Ronan Keating, who had flown in to lend his two pennies' worth. John and Edward had decided that another Backstreet Boys' hit – 'I Want It That Way' – could be their key to the final and launched into it, accompanied by a piano. Although the audition wasn't the worst they had ever done, a sudden case of nerves had overtaken the twins and after their performance, they left Louis and Ronan with a sorry feeling.

Immediately afterwards, both John and Edward were devastated as they told presenter Dermot O'Leary that they were sure they had messed up the audition and ruined their chances. A clearly upset Edward revealed: 'I was practically laughing at myself, imagining people looking at the TV and going, "Whoa, these guys are a joke!"' It was the first time that the public got to see the ever-confident twins let their guard down – underneath it all they seemed as insecure as the rest of the competitors.

'We're not a joke,' John insisted tearfully, 'we just wanted to do something different.'

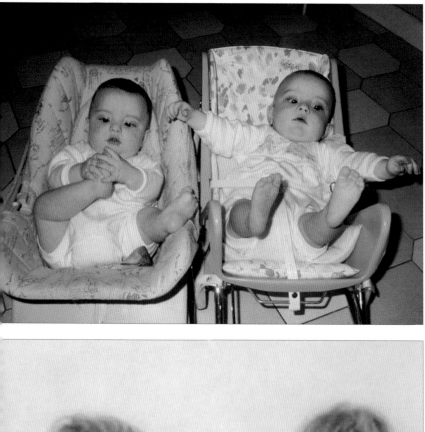

efore they were famous …

bove: Now, which one is which? John is on the left, Edward is on the right.

elow: Enjoying a bubble bath as toddlers.

Above left: Proud Grandfather James Grimes with a photo of the three Grimes grandsons.

Top right: The youngsters looking very smart.

Middle right: The boys relax at Christmas.

Below: Before the hair! John and Edward with a friend.

hind the scenes at *The X Factor*. The twins prepare for the show and, *ird row right*, Louis demonstrates that he too has the X factor. *Bottom ft*: Cheryl wishes the boys luck and, *bottom right*, Louis with Jedward's rents, Susanna and John.

Top: The boys meet Taboo, will.i.am and apl.de.ap from the Black Eyed Pea

Second row, left: Having a laugh with Peaches Geldof.

Second row, right: Making sure that they are up to speed with Louis' rules!

Third row, left: With Louis and Joe McElderry, 2009's *X Factor* winner.

Third row, right: Getting psyched up for a performance.

Bottom row, left: With the lovely Lucie Jones.

Bottom row, right: Louis finds out what the magazines have been saying about the boys.

ing what they
e best – entertaining
fans.

Who you gonna call? The famous *Ghostbusters* number.

Everybody loves Jedward! One of the boys is almost swallowed up by the fans.

A dream gig – Jedward backstage with Louis prior to supporting Westlife at Croke Park.

But they were right to worry: Ronan Keating for one was not sold on the youngsters from Dublin. He told Louis: 'They should have the most chemistry between all of these acts: they are twins, they have grown up together. But they look uncomfortable beside one another.' But Louis thought otherwise and stated: 'I think people will really like them.'

John and Edward then had an agonising wait of a couple of hours before they would discover if they were going home or going on to the *X Factor* live finals. Dermot O'Leary could see they were distressed and remarked that the boys were 'worrying more than any other group.' Indeed, the boys cried on camera and told him that they were terrified of 'just going home and that's the end. We just did our best and it could have gone well, but it didn't – but it was better to just go for it.'

By the end of the day, Louis and Ronan had had to pick between just two acts – girl band Project A and John and Edward. As the boys went off to meet with Louis and Ronan for the second time, they were fighting back the tears and Edward admitted: 'We thought that would be the end of us; that he was going to tell us to go home. When we were walking up there, we were already thinking about what we would tell everyone when we got back. The audition just seemed to have been like, really not good, so we wanted to just get it over with and get out of there. We were sad and thought it was all over.'

Louis too had an agonising couple of hours as he sought Ronan's advice over which groups he should pick as his final acts for the live shows. 'There was something about the twins from day one that I liked and I told Ronan that, but he really wasn't sold on them – I think he thought I was mad for even bringing them as far as Italy,' he remembers. 'But I could see that they were so nervous when they got to Italy – they weren't as confident as they had been, back at all the auditions. I just knew what was the right decision to make.'

When the moment came, John and Edward stood nervously in front of Louis – knowing that what he had to say next could change the paths of their lives forever, or have them back at a desk in school within a matter of weeks. Louis told them: 'On your first audition, I saw something in you guys that none of the other judges saw – I saw great potential. You reminded me of the early years of Boyzone and everyone said they were never going to make it and they made it, you know? There was a little bit of that with you guys. I do think you have something special, you know?'

He then went on to tell Project A how much he liked them: 'You have always been consistently good,' but added: 'I've thought long and hard about this. It's not good news – I'm sorry, you are going home.'

And so the twins were through and they could scarcely believe their ears. Both jumped over to Louis to give him a giant hug, and they were delighted when Dermot later told them: 'Louis believes in you.'

Their first call was to their mother Susanna, who was waiting anxiously by the phone to hear the news and screamed excitedly when her sons told her that they were on their way to the live shows.

'Everyone at home was so excited,' John recalls, 'I don't

think at that moment we knew that things were going to change so much – it was just like, "Yay, Louis didn't send us home!" We were glad that we didn't have to go back to school the next month and that we could just get preparing for the live show. Everyone was going to know our names – we just couldn't believe it.'

As things were looking better and better for the boys on the show, an online storm was brewing over bitter auditionees and viewers who had taken a dislike to them. Within a couple of weeks of John and Edward's first audition being broadcast on ITV, over 100,000 people had signed up to online groups branding them the worst *X Factor* singers ever. But the determined duo came out fighting straightaway and told the haters that they couldn't care less.

A defiant John declared: 'We are loving the whole experience – it's amazing! One of the best things about it is having people coming up to us in the streets. When Simon says that we are annoying, we just laugh. It's fine.'

As more and more people came out slamming their auditions, John and Edward continued to shrug off the negative comments. John said: 'We heard that the only thing worse than being talked about is not being talked about and we knew that when people got to see the real us on the show, the could change their minds. We didn't bother going online and all of that stuff to see what people had to say. We had made it through and were going to be singing on the live shows, so we had to just think about that – we had to concentrate.'

In late September 2009, John and Edward packed their

bags and left their parents for the first time. They were heading off to live in the *X Factor* house and master their very first routine ahead of the live shows. The boys were picked up by members of the show and taken to a plush pad in London that was to be their home with the rest of the show's finalists for the foreseeable future.

Finally, their dream was coming true and as far as they were concerned, they were not going to let it slip through their fingers easily. 'At that time, I think we knew that this was a once-in-a-lifetime opportunity,' John recalls. 'It was like this was the time where we would prove everyone wrong and everyone who had ever given us hassle in school would now see us and we could be like, ha.'

Of course the twins insisted that they were put in the same room at the *X Factor* house in London and from day one, they were always up to mischief. Edward says: 'We would just like, go into the fridge and eat whatever was there and stuff because we thought, you know, that we were all in the same boat. And then some people would be giving out about us eating their things and we were kinda like, OK, let's all chill out a bit here.'

As soon as fans started finding out where the plush *X Factor* house was located, they began to gather outside the building from dawn until dusk and the names that they were chanting the loudest were John and Edward's.

'There were these blinds and we weren't meant to look out the other side of them,' Edward grins. 'But me and John always did, and we would always wave and see there were loads of fans there for us, so that was really cool.'

Given their boarding-school background, neither John

nor Edward was very homesick – either way, they soon found out that they would not have much time to be yearning for creature comforts. From day one in the house, dance classes and singing lessons were the order of the day and if they had thought that this was going to be some sort of showbiz holiday camp, they were in for a big surprise.

'I remember that when we got in there with all of the others, some of them would just be talking about how lucky they were to get that far, and talking about getting kicked out on the first week, but for me and Edward, it was never like that,' John shrugs. 'We always saw the bigger picture and we weren't there as some sort of joke – we were already thinking about getting to the final and wanted to get bigger and better every single week. No way were we going to jinx things by saying that we might get kicked out on the first night – it's all about positive thinking, you guys!'

And before the live shows had even begun, the boys were getting fan mail by the bucket-load delivered to the X Factor house and to the ITV studios in the UK. The producers had never seen such a reaction to an act on the show.

While cowards were getting behind online campaigns against the twins, John and Edward were gathering thousands of fans all around the country, who just could not get enough of them. Louis Walsh remembers getting a phone call from workers on the show, telling him that the boys were shaping up to be a sensation.

'I knew that they were going to get people talking from the beginning,' he insists. 'But who could have known just how much they would be talking about them? I think that they were the most talked-about thing on the show for months.'

Every evening, the overwhelmed duo took time out to read their fan mail after spending hours trying to get to grips with their gruelling routines for the live shows. As well as their own number and a possible sing-off performance, all the X Factor acts would now have to rehearse a live number to be sung on the Sunday night shows. The contestants had never been under so much pressure, with so much to learn in just seven days.

Even though John and Edward were fighting fit and full of energy, they too found the days of constant rehearsals exhausting. 'I think we got a bit of a shock with all of the choreography and jumping around, and then trying to remember the words and make our voices sound good at the same time,' John admits. 'I remember just coming home every night and our heads would be spinning and we would be in the room trying to remember every move.

'From the beginning, we got loads of choreography and some of the other acts just had to stand there and sing. But we knew that all of that was going to make our performance better and we were willing to go that extra mile.'

Another adjustment that the twins had to make was getting used to having their every move snapped by the paparazzi. Even though they had spent nights awake in bed, talking about what it must be like to be chased by photographers, they were shell-shocked when it actually happened.

One of the first occasions when they were 'papped' was when they were preparing for the live shows and popped out to the shops to buy some cereal to eat. 'I don't think that we even thought they would be there,' Edward grins. 'We just went down to the shop like we had been doing for all of our lives, but there was photographers running after us and calling our names and they didn't know which of us was which. We loved it!

'I think that was when we started doing the peace sign and we have been doing it in photographs ever since – it's kind of cool to bring that back.'

John, Edward and the rest of the contestants were also introduced to some VIP treatments that they would become used to in the run-up to the live shows. As well as taking a trip to get their teeth whitened, they were escorted to the hairdresser's to have highlights. Wardrobe designers from *The X Factor* also worked closely with the boys to get a sense of their style while preparing their costumes for the TV show.

Edward admits: 'It all felt really cool, like this VIP treatment was what we had been waiting for – and we loved it. But we knew that it wasn't that important and was just part of the show, and we had to remain down-to-earth.

'I mean, like everyone likes to get free stuff and get pampered though, don't they? We enjoyed all of it!'

chapter six

THE LIVE SHOW ROLLERCOASTER

IN EARLY OCTOBER 2009, John and Edward met with choreographer Brian Friedman, vocal coach Evie and the rest of the team who were going to help them put together their very first performance.

'I remember meeting Brian and just being like, "What's Britney like?" because he taught her dance moves and is just amazing and like, the best dance instructor in the world,' John says. 'I think at the start we were a bit over-the-top and thinking that we could pull off all these mad dance moves on stage while singing a song – we didn't really know how hard it was to sing and dance all at the same time. Then we had to learn where all the cameras were and all of this, and he said he wanted us to lower ourselves onto the stage on ropes – that was pretty cool.'

The boys and the other finalists spent up to 10 hours a day rehearsing for their very first show and never far from the twins' mind was the fact that they could have been sent home on that very first night. 'We always said from the very start that you have to give it everything as if it is the last chance that you are ever going to get up there,' Edward says. 'Nobody ever knew who was going home – we just wanted to get up there and show everyone what we had, but we were nervous because we knew that people at home were not able to vote.

'We were wondering if anyone in England was going to like us and felt like we had to work really hard because we weren't from there and just wanted people to like us.'

Week One finally arrived and John and Edward were thrilled when they found out what their first performance was going to be. It was over three months since they had travelled to London for that very first audition – the dream was becoming a reality.

The Lucan students were preparing to take to the stage in front of a live television audience of anything up to 15 million. For two young boys from a country of less than 5 million, this was hard to believe – and the idea barely sank in. John admits: 'We kind of just went out there as if it was for the judges and the audience. I think if you think about gazillions of people, like, you might just pass out!'

WEEK ONE: 'ROCK DJ'

On Week One of the show, the boys sported black-and-white jackets and lowered themselves onto the stage from above for Robbie Williams' 'Rock DJ'. Louis and the twins had chosen the song as they saw it as the perfect blend of rap and singing to suit their voices. A number of hot backing dancers and an on-set DJ were brought in to give them a show-stopping starting night.

Just one minute into the routine, Simon Cowell could be spotted nodding and smiling away to the song.

Even though they were being beamed into the houses of over 12 million viewers, the duo showed no signs of nerves as they made their way confidently through the first song. A slight tone of booing from the crowd was soon drowned out by massive cheers from the studio audience: John and Edward had pulled it off on night one.

Judges' Comments: Week One

Dannii Minogue: 'You guys have got the whole country talking. I just want to say something: the girls told me from inside the house that you guys are very sweet, except when you steal their food from the fridge – I'm watching you! On the performance tonight, not the best vocals but a good performance and I loved the way that you entered.'

Cheryl Cole: 'I have to say, just from a personal point of view, I have got the most admiration for you two for even getting out here tonight. The stick you two have received over the last few weeks is unbelievable.

'You can't sing – fact, but you are up there giving it a go. You are young lads, it's not your fault that you are in the final twelve and good to you for coming out here tonight.'

Simon Cowell: 'I'm trying to find something here. For your age, I've got to hand it to you, you are amazingly thick-skinned – I'm going to give you that. I think to succeed in this business, you have got to have thick skin and that's the positives out of the way.

'It was a musical nightmare, the whole thing. I just had this thought of you winning the competition and what it would do: it would be a disaster. The truth is that Louis has put you through because you are Irish.'

Louis Walsh: (Louis was quick to jump to the twins' defence and told Simon that people in Ireland couldn't even vote). 'Yes, I did take a chance,' he shrugged, 'and I'm glad. Hey, on that performance, you were entertaining. I don't like that people in the press are giving you a hard time, who have never met you.

'I know you, and I know that you are really nice people and I want people to vote to keep you in – even just to annoy Simon. And you know, guys, not all bands in the charts are great singers.'

WEEK TWO: 'OOPS!... I DID IT AGAIN'

Many of the naysayers were sure that Jedward would be first to get the boot in Week One, but John and Edward's streak of luck continued when they managed to make it through to Week Two. In fact, the twins were the first contestants to have their names called out from the stage by Dermot O'Leary. A deadlock in voting finally resulted in gorgeous girl group Kandy Rain getting the boot, while the Grimes twins were laughing all the way to Week Two of the live finals.

But there was no rest for the wicked and the twins were up bright and early the next morning to get working on their second routine. This time they were over the moon when they discovered that they would be covering Britney Spears' 'Oops!... I Did It Again' on the show.

It was Divas Week, and John and Edward wanted to showcase their favourite diva song – with a Jedward twist. Sporting red latex suits and accompanied by yet another troupe of dancers, the twins took to the stage in their most difficult routine to date. Not only had Brian Friedman given them a number of complicated dance moves, he also upped the game by introducing props for them to work with on stage.

But John and Edward were not fazed: they had even suggested they be allowed to improvise the section where Britney talks to her boyfriend and had the judges in stitches with their own take on the cringe-worthy moment.

> John: 'Edward, before you go, I want to give you something.'
> Edward: 'Ah, it's beautiful. But I thought the old lady dropped it into the ocean?'
> John: 'Well, Edward, I went down and got it for you.'
> Edward: 'Ah, you shouldn't have.'

Fire explosions and top-class graphics were also added to the routine to ensure the twins brought another showstopper before the judges. Louis Walsh was absent attending the funeral of tragic Boyzone star Stephen Gately, 33, in Dublin, but the pair managed to win the other three judges around – well, sort of!

Judges' Comments: Week Two

Dannii Minogue: 'Boys, it's a big week for you guys. Louis is not here with you guys, so we know how tough that is. I have to say that honestly, vocally, it's not right but it's OK. The double divas from Dublin – I wish Louis was here! The good news is that it's entertaining, it's fun: it made Cheryl laugh.'

Cheryl Cole: 'I have to say that when it comes to a Saturday night, the act that I am most looking forward to is you two. Whether it's right or wrong, you are thoroughly entertaining and I hope you stay in longer – even if it's just to annoy Simon!'

Simon Cowell: 'Well, my initial reaction was "What the bloody hell was that?" Look guys, arguably – actually no, not arguably, the worst live performance I have ever sat through in all these years of doing the show. But I am going to give you this, in the same way I reacted to the first time I watched *The Exorcist*: I didn't like it, but I wanted to watch it again. That's sort of how I feel about you. To be fair to you, even though I was appalled by the performance, I do actually like you now as people because you are living on another planet, somewhere else entirely but sort of entertaining in a weird way.'

Even though the judging panel seemed to be warming to Jedward, the competition was getting tougher and John and Edward were counting on the public to keep them in for another week. With just 11 finalists left, Dermot slowly read out the roll call of contenders who had made it through to the next week. One by one they left the stage until only John and Edward remained with Rikki and Rachel Adedeji.

The twins were in luck once again when their names were read out, while Rachel and Rikki were left to battle it out in the sing-off. Rikki's rendition of Westlife's 'Flying Without Wings' was not enough to save him and he was eventually sent home by Simon's deciding vote.

After the show, a clearly gutted Cheryl remarked: 'I can't believe John and Edward are still in and Rikki is going home.'

Behind the scenes, John and Edward were beginning to feel a cold front from some of the other contestants. What was worse, the booing that they had received in the audience when they got through to the next round was the loudest it had been yet. But the duo were determined that both them and their fast-growing hairdos would rise above the naysayers.

Edward admitted both he and John were really beginning to feel the pressure after Week Two, while John says: 'It felt like people thought it was funny that we got through Week One and then they were wondering why we were still there after Week Two. We felt like a lot of people were misunderstanding us and there were so many haters. So many people seemed to be spending so much time hating Jedward and we just wanted to sing and entertain.'

Even though the online campaign against them was growing, on the ground the twins had an ever-increasing fan base watching their every move. One morning, just a couple of days into their stay at the luxurious *X Factor* house, the boys were woken by the sound of fans chanting their name.

According to John: 'That was the most amazing feeling. We went to the window and waved down at them, and they had posters and were screaming. We could not believe it. So then, every time we came back from rehearsals or whatever, we would try to get over to the gate to talk to them and they would go really crazy. It felt like we had made it.'

WEEK THREE: 'SHE BANGS'

There was little time for rest as John and Edward had to get working on yet another gruelling routine for Week Three and after receiving pretty positive overall comments from Dannii, Cheryl and Simon in Week Two, they were determined to put on another showstopper.

'She Bangs' by Ricky Martin was the song of choice and Jedward were once again looking to put their own stamp on the Latin singer's hit. This time, sexy backing dancers were brought in to get into the groove with the boys, who were not complaining.

The twins spent up to eight hours a day rehearsing for Week Three in the knowledge that as each week moved on, the tougher the competition was getting tougher. Edward revealed that both he and John were going to give it their all: 'You just don't know which performance is going to be your last so you have to make it a good one.'

Once again, Susanna and John made the journey over from Dublin to watch their sons. Susanna admitted:

'Watching John and Edward on the show every week makes us so proud. This is what they have always wanted.'

Guest mentor for Week Three was crooner Michael Bublé, who admitted that he couldn't help but get on with the twins: 'It's hard not to like the kids because they are really nice kids. They were dancing their little butts off, too.'

Before the show Simon Cowell declared that he would leave the country if John and Edward went on to win, but the carefree twins refused to let him get them down. On the night, the wardrobe department kitted them out in wacky lime green and dark pink suits with tailored white shirts.

Louis introduced Jedward as 'the act everyone wants to see' and once again, it was show time. John and Edward entered the stage by running down through the live studio audience, catching people off-guard from the very beginning. It was Big Band Night and with the support of their troupe of sexy dancers and inflatable caricatures of themselves, Jedward were confident the judges would be impressed.

Judges' Comments: Week Three

Cheryl Cole: 'Do you know what? You are two of the nicest kids I have ever met. I think the booing tonight… just don't take it on board, right? Do you know what? You are fast becoming my guilty pleasure! Every week I can't wait to see what you come out with next.'

Simon Cowell: 'I don't know if I can do this anymore. OK, let me try and be constructive here – and I'm struggling.

Look, if you heard it on the radio it would probably be one of the worst things you have ever heard but I give you some credit for at least putting on a show and having fun. But then I take it back to being a singing competition and this is appalling!'

Louis Walsh: 'It is a TV show and we are never going to please all of the people all of the time. Simon signed an act once called Zig and Zag – these boys are better and boys: you are getting better, week by week! Some people like you and some people are really rude, and they are in the audience booing and that's what it's all about.'

John and Edward were quick to hit back at Cowell, while John had Louis on his feet when he said: 'The first thing that I want to say is: "Simon, thanks for the dance moves."' But backstage, both the boys were once again worried that their time might be up. 'I don't think anyone was ever totally sure that they were going through – you never knew,' admits John. 'You had to wait until the next night and it just seemed like the longest twenty-four hours of your life.'

Only two of Louis' groups now remained – Miss Frank and John and Edward. John stood on stage with his arm around his brother as Dermot O'Leary slowly listed out the finalists. Relief was clearly etched across the boys' faces as they were named the sixth act through to Week Four of the show but the boos from the crowd could not be ignored: this was getting serious.

At this stage, the twins' father John had had enough of

the constant stick that his sons were getting and spoke out in order to protect them. On the whole, John and Susanna had avoided media interviews while John and Edward were on the show because they wanted to let their boys shine by themselves but, before long, things were getting too much for their parents to take and their father wanted to put an end to it.

'It was difficult to watch them getting a hard time. Some of the things said were vicious and as parents, it knocks you for six,' he revealed. 'There's been booing and that's been tough because they are so young. The first week the boys were on the show, they were shocked at all the hate campaigns on the Internet, but they've grown in confidence now – they take it all with a pinch of salt.

'They haven't been reduced to tears and I would be surprised if they were. They were born to do this, but at the same time they know it's entertainment and don't take it too seriously: they are determined to enjoy it.'

In November 2009, Louis Walsh also admitted that the hostility towards the twins was getting to their parents. 'Of course it is hard for them to sit there week after week and listen to all that. They were worried about the boys, but I think they know that we are looking after them well and John and Edward are happy.

'They are not letting any of this get to them – they are so determined and their parents can see that they want to be here. They don't let any of that get them down but you can understand why John and Susanna were worried. It's a tough industry but these boys are tough.'

Asked if he thought that the twins could win the series,

Louis said: 'I don't know, it's up to the people at home. I would love to get two more weeks with them. You know, there's some really good talent left. I'm happy that I've got this far.'

The boys found themselves on the front pages yet again when an online video sparked controversy among YouTube users that the twins had been handpicked to win *The X Factor* before it had even begun. One Irish hopeful had captured John and Edward briefly in the nine-minute video about contestants who had travelled to London to audition, but the show's producers claimed that Jedward initially auditioned in Glasgow.

Online conspiracy theorists felt that the duo must have been handpicked by producers in London to sail through the auditions in Glasgow, but ITV and *The X Factor* were quick to deny any talk of a 'fix' involving the twins. A spokesperson said: 'There is always a pre-audition in front of the judges. They did a pre-audition in London, where they were asked to audition for the judges. They were given a choice of Glasgow or London; they couldn't make London so they went to Glasgow.'

Adding fuel to that week's rumours that the twins were being set up for victory, the mother of *X Factor* hopeful Lloyd Daniels came out and said that attacks on the twins by Simon Cowell were backfiring. Lisa Daniels told a local newspaper: 'If John and Edward do a good performance entertainment-wise and Simon says something nasty to them, their fans double and triple vote just to keep them in. It's quite worrying, but then again, it's an open competition.'

The twins' mentor Louis Walsh was quick to come out

and slam any notion of fixes concerning the boys. He said: 'The fact of the matter is I had a battle to even get them on the show. Everybody thought that I was crazy but I could see something in them from the start.

'Simon doesn't pretend to be against people – if he doesn't like you, he doesn't like you. John and Edward went through the same audition process as everyone else and are here because I could see something there – it is as simple as that.'

WEEK FOUR: 'WE WILL ROCK YOU'

Rock Week saw John and Edward take on the Five version of the classic Queen hit. With great rock singers like Jamie Afro competing against them, they would really have to find their inner rock gods to win over both the public and the judges.

After being told by Cheryl the previous week that they were 'fast becoming her guilty pleasure', the twins were determined to wow everyone once again. 'I think last week's performance was our best performance to date,' observed John. 'We are enjoying ourselves on stage and are having the most fun out of everyone.

'Outside of the house, it has been the craziest week, with fans everywhere. But I think that with Rock Week it can be me and Edward's week because it's all about the performance and rocking it out on stage.'

That week, a number of front-page stories had appeared in the press tipping John and Edward to go on and win the show. One person that was not happy was judge Simon Cowell, who declared: 'It goes beyond nightmares, because nightmares, you can wake yourself up from. I think Louis' luck runs out tonight and I cannot wait!'

Meanwhile, John and Edward shrugged off Simon's comments and took to the stage ready to give their most high-energy performance to date. Armed with eye-liner, biker boots and floor-length leather jackets, the lads were set to rock and they didn't disappoint – making their way through the rap-influenced Five version and mastering a difficult crowd-surfing move that choreographer Brian Friedman had set for them.

On the judging panel, Louis was loving it and bopped along to the beat while Cheryl, Dannii and Simon looked on smiling.

The boys had managed to do it again.

Judges Comments: Week Four

Dannii Minogue: 'It is Halloween and that was quite scary! I think you almost needed a Sat Nav to find your way back to where the lyrics were. I do look forward to seeing you every week, but I'm not sure that I would look forward to hearing you on the radio.

'Do you know what I mean? You have really got to listen to the song.'

Cheryl Cole: 'The production was fantastic. You are definitely dressed for the occasion – Halloween. Yeah, I felt like I was rocking to that song.'

Simon Cowell: 'It was Night of the Living Dead – singing Queen out of tune, possibly destroying Queen's career forever. Guys, I'll credit you with tenacity – you have stayed in the competition, you are thick-skinned – however, you cannot defend that singing tonight, Louis.'

Louis Walsh: 'Simon, it's all about the show! These are two young kids living the dream – they are having fun. The audience love them – they are energetic, they are entertaining and they are exciting. This is what the music industry is all about.'

Asked how they come on week after week to face a barrage of criticism, John and Edward admitted: 'We have just got to take it with a pinch of salt and take on the chin and improve.'

WEEK FIVE: 'GHOSTBUSTERS'

With each week that passed, choreographer Brian Friedman admitted that he had to think long and hard about Jedward's routine. Every week that they stayed in meant that their upcoming performance had to top all of the previous ones. Since Week One, he had been bowled over by John and Edward and wanted to bring out the very best in them.

'You know, they are just such nice kids that I always wanted to get them to reach their potential,' he revealed. 'They were just hilarious to work with and we had the most fun together. Each week was a blast but I think that "Ghostbusters" week was special.'

Louis and the crew decided that the theme tune from the 1980s TV show would be just perfect for John and Edward to perform on Week Five: Movie Week. And if their sets had been impressive in the past, Week Five was to be the icing on the cake.

Set designers worked tirelessly to build the twins a classic car, which would be lowered down from the ceiling for their grand entrance. The wardrobe department was also flat out designing various costumes for ghouls and goblins that would take over the stage during John and Edward's set. And the twins themselves were beyond excited about their upcoming performance.

'I think that "Ghostbusters" was one of our favourites,' Edward admits. 'There was just so much going on and we had so much fun in rehearsals all week. It was like being in theatre or something because there was so much going on.'

John added: 'I think that one of the differences between me and Edward and other people on the show was that we put so much into our performances. Other people just had to stand there and sing, but we had these big productions with cars and monsters, and acting and everything. With us, it was more of a show than anything else – there was so much going on onstage.'

Jedward entered the stage looking like Zig and Zag, their heads bopping from side to side inside their *Ghostbusters* car – and the audience went wild. It was the boys' most outrageous performance yet; perfect Saturday night entertainment. Indeed, the clip of Jedward's performance in Week Five went on to garner more views on YouTube than any of the other finalists' pieces.

John and Edward blasted the monsters with their ghost-busting guns and got a giggle from the judges when

Edward screamed, 'John, save me!' to which his brother replied: 'Don't be such a baby.'

Judges' Comments: Week Five

Dannii Minogue: 'I've honestly got no idea of anything constructive to say. It's a singing competition – you either talk or you rap so I am wondering what you are going to say if you win the competition. I love watching you guys perform but I can't imagine listening to you on the radio.

Cheryl Cole: 'Do you know what? You bring fun to this show. Whether people like you or whether they don't, it's fun to watch. Kids from like, three to 10 absolutely adore you, so good on you!'

Simon Cowell: 'Look guys, I think we have established over the past few weeks that you can't sing but this was actually a good song for you – actually you did choose the right song for them, Louis. Based on some of the horrors we have seen from them before, this was sort of good – in a very childish average age of one and a half, enjoying things. I thought it was more entertaining than some of the karaoke stuff I've seen before, so well done.'

Louis Walsh: 'Guys, all I know is everywhere I go people are talking about Jedward. You are two guys, every week you come out smiling and happy. I haven't had one problem with you. The world is full of doom and gloom, and these boys are having fun – that's what this show is all about: fun!'

Presenter Dermot O'Leary went on to praise Jedward for getting as close as they were going to get to a compliment from Simon Cowell.

'It's so cool that we come out here and normally it's like, oh not you two,' said John. 'But it was a good comment, Simon. Thumbs-up!'

O'Leary then asked how they felt about getting booed and bad comments from the judges and Edward told him 'You just go for it. You just have fun and go out on stage. You just go with the opportunity and do it.'

The boys then called on their fans to give them support and said: 'We are not safe. Only for them we wouldn't be here.'

Jedward returned to the *X Factor* house again that night, hopeful their dream was not coming to an end. Sunday saw the return of all the groups to the London studio for the results show. The mood backstage was good and there was huge excitement as the Black Eyed Peas and Leona Lewis were the guest performers on the night. John and Edward were thrilled when they got to meet the band backstage and even spent some time chatting with Will.i.am. The legendary singer told them: 'Always believe in your ability. Don't take someone's opinion and let it crush you.'

'That meant a lot to me and Edward,' John admitted. 'He is in one of the biggest bands in the world and he doesn't let what people say get him down. When he said that, we really wanted to be that way too.'

The pair watched excitedly from backstage as the Black Eyed Peas and Leona Lewis performed, but tension was building about that night's results show: John and Edward's nightmares were about to become a reality.

One by one, Dermot O'Leary called out the names of the acts that had made it through. In the end, it came down to John and Edward and Welsh beauty Lucie Jones – Jedward were going to have to give the performance of their lives in the sing-off to stay on the show.

The boys chose to go with their favourite song from *The X Factor* – 'Rock DJ' – in the hope of keeping their spot. The energetic performance was the first time for weeks that John and Edward were on the stage without props or dancers but they delivered and finished off with high kicks into the audience.

Lucie too gave a show-stopping performance and it was left in the hands of the judges to decide who was going home. Louis was the first to give his verdict and said: 'I thought, Lucie, you were absolutely incredible and there's no way you should have been in the bottom two, girl – no way. But Lucie, I do mentor the boys so I have to save them and I have to send you home.'

Next up was Lucie's own mentor Dannii Minogue, who nailed her colours firmly to the Lucie mast, saying: 'The act that I'm sending home tonight is John and Edward.'

Cheryl Cole was next and said: 'I just want to say that before I say me decision [sic], that over the past few weeks I have really come to love you two guys. You are really lovely lads and I have loved getting to know you, but tonight I am going to send John and Edward home.'

The decision now lay with Simon Cowell. If he picked Jedward, the boys' journey was over. But if he went with

Lucie, the decision would go to deadlock and be decided by the public vote.

'Well,' Simon shrugged. 'It's a tricky one. I'm not surprised by the way, first of all, that both of you are in the bottom two. Having said that, I don't think either of you can win – I don't.

'I think, Lucie, my problem with you is that I believe there is a ceiling and I think with John and Edward, we've had some horrific performances. Having said that, who would I rather see again? I would probably rather see the boys, I would.

'I got a lot of stick last week for taking it down to the public vote and I think I am going to do it again: I'm going to let the public decide.'

Jedward were close to tears as the voting went to deadlock – as was Lucie. In all the years of X Factor, this was one of the most nail-biting moments of them all. Half the audience cheered for loudly for John and Edward, while the rest were up for gorgeous Lucie.

Two minutes later, Dermot O'Leary made one of the most shocking announcements of the show: Jedward had received more votes and so John and Edward would live to fight another day. The shell-shocked twins hugged Lucie as Dannii Minogue put her face in her hands.

Louis, needless to say, was thrilled. John and Edward had managed to avoid the axe, while Lucie was on her way back to Wales.

The young girl was gracious in defeat and jumped to the defence of the twins as soon as she learned that she would be going home, saying: 'I'm gutted, but the boys deserve to be there – they work harder than anyone.'

Meanwhile, in a dig at the Grimes' vocal ability, Lucie's mentor Dannii Minogue blasted: 'I just wish all the singers good luck in the singing competition. It shouldn't have happened!'

But the trouble was only just beginning for the show's boss, Simon Cowell. A massive 3,000 people went on to complain to ITV, blasting Cowell's 'outrageous' decision to let the decision go to the public vote. But he was standing by his choice and happy to leave John and Edward to fight another day: 'People always like to disagree with me, but I knew this would be more controversial than usual. There will be people who are Lucie fans and think she should have been given a chance.'

The boys were left in tears after booing from the audience and host Holly Willoughby asked them if they feared a backlash following the controversial vote. Edward admitted neither he nor John really knew what was going on: 'It was just really hard to be in the bottom two and give it everything up there. We thought that we would be gone – it was a bit of a rollercoaster.'

Backstage, tensions were equally high with judge Dannii Minogue making a beeline for Simon Cowell as soon as the cameras stopped rolling. Dannii was devastated that her act got the boot and told Simon exactly what she taught of his decision to let the vote go to deadlock.

Following the results show, John and Edward looked jaded as they made their way back to Louis' dressing room. The boys had burst into tears after learning that they would be the ones to remain in the show.

A host of guests had flown in from Ireland to watch the

show from Louis' dressing room – including yours truly. As John and Edward entered the room they were greeted with cheers and a hug from their mentor, but both of them looked shell-shocked.

'We really liked Lucie and don't want people to hate us because of this,' John admitted. 'She was so talented and had like, a really good voice and it was just hard up there. We felt like everyone was a little bit against us – after everything that Simon said, we can't believe that he chose to save us.'

Meanwhile, Louis was on hand to tell John and Edward to put the night behind them and concentrate on the next week. Their parents John and Susanna made their way backstage as soon as possible after watching the boys go through the ordeal on live television. Both John and Edward took some time with their family before heading back to the *X Factor* house that night.

'It's getting harder as every week goes on and the amount of people in the house gets smaller,' Edward observed. 'When it came down to the vote, we looked at Simon and were sure we were going home. Like, I don't think that anyone thought we were going to be staying – I thought I was hearing things.'

As a storm of controversy continued to brew that night, fellow finalist Daniel Johnson jumped to the defence of the twins. Speaking backstage, he said: 'They are two great guys and we all think so much of them. Things would not be the same without John and Edward. I can't believe that this booing is still going on. I get it too and it's heartbreaking to hear. John and Edward just keep those smiles on their faces, though – they are incredible.'

For the rest of that week Simon Cowell was under pressure from fans claiming that he let the vote go to deadlock because he knew Jedward would go through. But the show's boss slammed such reports as 'nonsense'.

'I didn't think either could win, so it seemed fair to let the public have their say,' he insisted. 'But I had no idea how the public vote had gone – I never get told what the figures are. I always make my decision based on what I have seen, not on what I want to happen.'

Meanwhile, Louis Walsh was thrilled that his remaining act had managed to stay in the show and stated that Jedward were 'the real stars of X Factor 2009.'

'This week is only going to make them stronger: the more people knock John and Edward, the more they come back fighting,' he declared. 'These guys are what Saturday night TV is all about and this is only the beginning. Everyone loves them, from kids to parents. Everywhere I go, people are asking about them. They have huge careers ahead of them and people are already lining up to sign them – John and Edward have a huge career ahead of them.

'I love working with them because they make me laugh and the show just would not be the same without them. Everyone on the show loves them – from the crew to the other contestants.'

With just seven acts now remaining, Jedward were closer than ever to winning the title of X Factor 2009. The Lucan lads had managed to make it from over 200,000 hopefuls to the final seven. Alongside Olly Murs, Jamie Archer, Danyl Johnson, Lloyd Daniels and Stacey Solomon, the twins were now household names in Ireland and the UK.

But if they were going to keep living the dream, they would have to put all the controversy from Week Five behind them and get their confidence back up.

WEEK SIX: 'UNDER PRESSURE'

With the arrival of Queen Week, it seemed that Jedward were once again in luck. The Classic Queen song, 'Under Pressure', was to be theirs for Week Six – but with a twist. The show's producers decided that a remix of Vanilla Ice's 'Ice Ice Baby' in the middle of the song could give it that extra zest.

After hours of rehearsals, the boys were feeling confident – finally, they had found a song that they really felt at home with. In their video diary for that week, John and Edward admitted that they had been sure that they were on the way back to Ireland the previous week. 'We were in the bottom two and we thought we were going home and I was like, come on, John, let's just perform and end on a high note,' said Edward. 'Now we get to come back again and do a really exciting performance, thanks to all you guys! We didn't even plan our second song. I was backstage and the Black Eyed Peas were there and they were like, come on guys!'

John added: 'I think to be a successful group or be a world renowned artist like The Backstreet Boys, Black Eyed Peas or Robbie Williams, they have all been the nicest people and I think to make it anywhere in the music business, it's all about being a nice person.'

Their entry to the stage involved jumping through a huge graffiti sign that read: 'John and Edward'. Disaster was narrowly averted when Edward stumbled on their grand entrance in front of millions of viewers. Thankfully, he managed to find his feet and slip back into the routine before many people noticed.

The rap was a stroke of unexpected genius and had the live audience screaming for more. Wearing shiny grey suits, John and Edward looked more at home on stage than ever before. Their singing was improved and their rapping flawless – and they had managed to master the complicated dance moves Brian Friedman had assigned them.

Disaster was once again very narrowly averted when Calvin Harris stormed the stage and started to dance around with a pineapple on his head. The singer also brandished his backside at the audience and was later thrown out of the theatre by the show's security. Although John and Edward looked somewhat stunned, they didn't let the unexpected arrival of Calvin with his pineapple head put them off and managed to get to the end of their routine in one piece.

Judges' Comments: Week Six

Dannii Minogue: 'Let me ask you, Louis: for the rule book, where does Vanilla Ice fit in with Queen week?'

Louis Walsh: 'It is a Queen song, though, Dannii and they were great.'

Dannii: 'OK – so there's Louis' rules and everyone else's rules – I'm sorry, some of that rapping was even out of time.'

Cheryl Cole: 'Do you know what? I am so happy to hear them chanting "Jedward" for once. There's no boos – they are all going mad for you – it's lovely to hear. Over the past few weeks, you come out here, you put on a hard exterior and we kind of forget that actually, you are 17-year-old lads with an opportunity and you are running with it. Good for you! You are entertaining and I thoroughly enjoyed it.'

Simon Cowell: 'I'm sort of understanding this a little bit more now. I can't judge you in the real world – I have to judge you in Jedwardland wherever that planet exists. If I kind of take myself there, I would say that was your best performance yet.

'I have to say this: there's no point in getting angry or serious about this – if people like you, they like you. I want to say this as well: you have conducted yourselves very well in this competition because you haven't whined – you have just got on with it.

Louis Walsh: 'Boys, this was your best performance – it was the most authentic performance. You look like pop stars and when the idiot jumped up from the audience, it didn't even faze you guys. I want everybody to please lift the phone and vote for Jedward – I need the votes!'

Jedward were understandably thrilled with the feedback they got from the judges. And the audience even managed to drown out Dannii Minogue's comments while cheering for them. It certainly was a case of 'what a difference a week makes' and public opinion now seemed to be swaying very much in favour of the twins.

'I think that overall, we were most confident after the Queen performance,' John observed. 'Even if we were to go home that night, the judges had given us positive comments, the audience were cheering really loud and we loved every minute of it – it was one of our favourite shows from the whole series.'

Yet again, Jedward faced a wait of over 24 hours before learning if Week Six was to be their last on the show. That Sunday's *X Factor* got off to a kicking start with all of the contestants coming together to perform 'Bohemian Rhapsody'. The finalists were then joined on stage by Queen legends Brian May and Roger Taylor.

Next up was hip-shaking hottie Shakira, who spun the studio into a tizzy with a performance of her new single. But as usual, everyone – including John and Edward – just wanted to hear the results.

First out of the hat to go through to the next week was Joe McElderry, followed by Danyl, Stacey and Olly Murs. For a moment it looked as if John and Edward were destined for another week in the bottom two – until their names were called out.

Louis jumped out of his chair as John and Edward once again defied the critics and sailed through to Week Seven. It seemed the Jedward bubble was never going to burst. Queen and Vanilla Ice had come up trumps for the twins, while Jamie Afro got the boot.

Earlier that Sunday, John and Edward took some time out from their hectic schedule for an appearance on *Sky*

News. The fact that the huge news organisation had requested them – and none of the other acts – for interview was another indication of their ever-growing popularity.

The journalist began by asking the twins how they were coping with their critics. Speaking from outside the studio in Wembley, John revealed: 'We are just having a great time – we are live? We just can't believe that we are on *The X Factor*: we just go out there every single week and have the most fun of our lives. We never just stand there and go, oh my God, I'm on *The X Factor*! We just give it our all every week.'

An excited Edward added: 'We are on *Sky News*, guys, come on!'

Asked about the 'pretty severe criticism' they had been having, Edward admitted: 'Yeah, I feel like our main focus is just to go out there and do our performance. Major artists, they all get criticism and it all comes with it. We would not have entered this competition if we weren't expecting that: we don't let it get us down.'

When asked if they thought that the last night had been their best performance yet, John admitted: 'It's just about going out there every single week and just having fun. It's not about taking it too seriously because if you are taking it too seriously, you are not enjoying it. It's about making the most of it and you are meeting all of these cool people – all of these celebrities who are just so down-to-earth – and it's all about being like them and looking up to your idols.'

Edward went on to say that Louis Walsh had been pushing them further and further each week: 'He just tells us to go out there and just do it. He's like our friend – we get him, and he gets us; he's really cool with us. Last week, we were in the bottom two and we just had to go out there and give it our all, and we just had fun with it.'

The journalist then brought up the fact that a lot of people were questioning the boys' talent and saying they couldn't really sing. But John and Edward were by now polished at dealing with whatever questions were thrown their way and were ready for the challenge – even on live TV.

John hit back: 'I think the thing about me and Edward every single week, like I know that we are not these major opera singers or whatever, but we just go out there and we have fun. It's all about performance and about your stage presence because the thing about Freddie Mercury was he was so unique and so… he was Freddie Mercury. It was all about the performance and all about the vocals. It's all about everything.

'You have to go out every single week and give it your all – it's about different aspects. People want to come to a concert and see people having fun; it's not about just standing there.'

He also admitted he knew neither he nor Edward were 'the most amazing singers' but added: 'at least we give it a try. The best singers out there aren't the most amazing singers but everybody loves them.'

The twins even went on to provide a quick snippet from their 'Under Pressure' performance to the cameraman – live and without prior knowledge – proving that they were ready for anything the media had to throw at them. As they made their way through the rap, the thousands of waiting fans outside the studio cheered.

'We love them – we hope they will vote for us!' Edward beamed.

John became a bit overwhelmed at the end and gushed excitedly: 'I can't believe I am on *Sky News*. It's so cool – I mean, come *on*!'

Edward laughed: '*Sky News* guys… Hey Grandad, hey to all my family!'

That night, it seemed that the gods were once again smiling down on the Dublin boys. Rocker Jamie Archer was given his marching orders, while Jedward were through to Week Seven.

Londoner Jamie had been forced to go head to head with Lloyd Daniels in the sing-off and found himself on his way home. But it was a dream night for John and Edward, who also got to perform the Queen classic 'Bohemian Rhapsody' with the remaining contestants live on the show. The lads were thrilled when Queen guitarist Brian May then came out on stage and played while they made their way through the routine.

The dream was still very much alive and well: the Jedward bubble showed no sign of bursting.

Gossip was rife on TV shows and radio stations all over Ireland and the UK – could the boys really be in with a chance of winning the whole show? Nothing now seemed impossible where John and Edward were concerned.

In their Week Seven video diary, the boys revealed they could hardly believe that they had been on the show for nearly two months.

'This week has been the most intense week ever,' John told the diary. 'Last week we had one day to learn "Under Pressure" and Vanilla Ice, and it was crazy that we had to learn so many lyrics but we pulled it off on the night.

'We are so delighted that you guys voted for us yet again – another week and you kept us in!'

Edward added that they were gob-smacked when they came face to face with Shakira backstage at the show: 'The one and only – her hips don't lie.'

The twins also took the time to tell their fans that they did in fact like the name Jedward – which followers had begun to call them: 'I think people who call us Jedward, it's because sometimes they can't fit our full name on a T-shirt going across, so it's OK to write Jedward. But when you see us in public, it's kind of weird to come up and be like, "Hey, Jedward!"

'We don't mind because our fans came up with that name for us and it's cool if they want to call us Jedward because it's like the Jackson 5. It's OK with us.'

After getting through with their Queen/Vanilla Ice mash, John and Edward were thrilled to learn the producers had organised a trip back home for them. The twins sparked hysteria when they turned up at their old school in Dublin to perform on 17 July. Jedward made the surprise visit to their school early in the morning and stunned their teachers and classmates with an impromptu performance. Their classmates scrambled to get pictures and autographs, with one girl recalling how they used to sign their names on her copybook as if they were famous.

Jedmania gripped the school as news spread that the

boys were back in town for one day only. The twins were determined to fit in as much as possible on their one day back home and left the school after an hour.

Next up was the running track at University College Dublin, where they used to train with their athletics club in Dundrum before the show began. Hundreds of students legged it to the running track to catch a glimpse of the twins booting it around the field.

But the people that John and Edward were most looking forward to seeing was their granny and granddad – and all of their pets. After their public appearances, the twins were whisked off to a relative's house to meet up with their parents and grandparents. A huge media presence in their home of Lucan meant that a decoy had to be arranged so that the boys could enjoy some family time elsewhere.

Only a couple of months before, they had left home just two normal hopefuls trying out at *The X Factor* – now they couldn't even return to their own house for fear of a stampede.

Their thrilled parents was there to welcome the boys at the door and admitted that they were delighted at how well John and Edward had been doing on the show.

Mum Susanna said: 'John and myself are very proud of the boys and we are absolutely delighted that they have been doing so well.' Chuffed granddad Kevin added: 'John and Edward are my grandsons and I'm very proud of them.'

However, both the twins were alarmed at how people's attitudes back home had changed towards them within a matter of weeks. 'When you go home, you kind of think about how far you have come,' Edward mused. 'The last time we left we were no one and now everyone knows who we are. They gave us loads of spirit and pride.'

Plans for the boys to return to their house in Lucan had to be abandoned after hundreds of fans began to gather there. One rumour circulating was that they were planning a trip to their local supermarket that evening to meet fans. Within the space of one hour, hundreds had arrived, hoping to meet them. Radio stations across Dublin were broadcasting the news that John and Edward were expected to pop into Superquinn in Lucan, County Dublin. The bakery in the supermarket even whipped up a special cake to welcome the pair within an hour of learning that they were due to arrive. Sadly, for the hundreds of fans who had gathered, it was just a rumour gone out of control.

As John and Edward caught up with their loved ones away from the public, rumours were also spreading that they were going to arrive at Grafton Street in Dublin to turn on the Christmas lights. As thousands of eager fans gathered, hoping to catch a glimpse of the stars, the twins were already on their way to the airport and back to London. Their trip home had been short and sweet, but was just the boost that they needed after six weeks on the show.

One thing was for sure: they were both beginning to realise that they weren't just John and Edward Grimes from Lucan any more – they were a household name collectively known as Jedward.

Ironically, it seemed that the more controversy the twins

became reluctantly involved in, the more fans they acquired. Sack upon sack of fan mail was delivered to the X *Factor* house and ITV studios for the boys. Scrapbooks, CDs and long-winded letters from all over Ireland and the UK flooded in from girls, declaring their undying love for Jedward.

Between rehearsals, John and Edward spent hours going through all of their mail and writing back to as many fans as possible. One example of the pages of poetry they received is from mum-of-two Sandra Harris, who wrote of her devotion to the pair in a sonnet. The ode went:

> *'Course they're Jedward to the nation.*
> *They've done well to get this far. Though Simon*
> *hates them and says their singing's below par.*
> *In fact, he really hates them – he says he'll quit*
> *if Jedward win, but that just makes the public try*
> *even harder to keep them in.*

John and Edward were by now old pros when it came to keeping their female fans wanting more. In their Week Seven video diary, they described what they would like to do if they went out on a date.

John teased: 'Last week we said in our video diary that we would date one of our fans. I want to tell you guys what we would do, OK. We wouldn't do the whole typical thing, like going to a cinema or typical stereo things that everyone thinks you have to do: we would do something special – something completely different, fun – John and Edward style.'

WEEK SEVEN: 'BABY I'M YOUR MAN'

As the only group left in the competition, Jedward had the full attention of Louis Walsh, who was on call 24/7 to help them. And the pop manager was the first to admit that in Week Seven, he decided to give them their toughest song yet for George Michael Week.

Brian Friedman revealed: 'There's a lot of stuff being thrown at them – a lot of choreography. What I need for them is intense focus.'

And while Simon wondered whether Louis was now giving the twins too much to do, Walsh was confident they could handle the workload and said: 'John and Edward practise more than anyone else and I know, tonight, they are going to be fantastic.'

Wearing tight white trousers, white jackets and T-shirts with 'Choose Life' in pink Neon, Jedward hit the stage running and made their way confidently through the song.

Judges' Comments: Week Seven

Dannii Minogue: 'What really shocked me tonight was that the singing was in tune and the rapping was out of time, so I don't know what's happening now – I'm totally confused.'

Cheryl Cole: 'You two have been on the biggest and toughest rollercoaster out of everybody and no matter what happens from here on in, you should be really proud of yourselves for getting this far.'

Simon Cowell: 'I don't think it was George and Andrew –

it was Andrew and Andrew. Perfect song choice: I do think, however, that Louis is giving you too much to do. It's like he has turned you into his version of action men dolls – just every week giving them this crazy, crazy choreography.'

Louis Walsh: 'They never stop rehearsing. Everywhere I go this week there are young girls shouting, "Jedward, Jedward, Jedward!" These boys are connecting with the young people and I am having the best time of my life working with you. However, I need people to vote – I want people to vote. This show would not be the same without them: we would have no fun.'

Simon Cowell: 'You have converted a lot of people, you are like this unstoppable machine at the moment.'

But later the very next night, Simon's words proved to be ironic. The machine that was Jedward was going to have to shelve any dreams of winning the show that night for the end was nigh.

On Sunday night, John and Edward found themselves in the bottom two with popular contestant and close pal Olly Murs. They would have to give the performance of their lives to make it through another week. But ambitious crooner Olly was undoubtedly going to pull out all of the stops to keep himself in the competition and as he was Simon's act, Jedward knew it was highly unlikely that they would get Cowell's vote. But they had gotten this far and after a quick pep talk from Louis, John and Edward were more than willing to fight for their place on the show.

The sing-off was on, and John and Edward had just seconds to decide which number they were going to go with. In the aftermath of Boyzone star Stephen Gately's death, they decided that the band's hit single 'No Matter What' would be a fitting choice.

Nervously, the twins made their way through the song stripped of the backing dancers and choreographed routines that they were by now used to. It was just John, Edward and the song. But Olly Murs pulled out all the stops with his polished rendition of Eric Clapton's 'Wonderful Tonight' and in the end, when pitted against one of the show's favourites, the Grimes brothers had a feeling their time was up.

'I think we both kind of knew that it was the end,' John recalled. 'When we were up against Olly – like he was such an amazing singer – we kind of knew that we would be going home that night.'

And the twins' gut feeling was soon proved right.

Louis, of course, voted to keep his group in, but the other judges were to send them home. After voting for Olly to remain in the competition, Simon Cowell told Jedward: 'I'm actually going to miss you, I am. But obviously, I am going to stick with my artist for the right reasons.'

Cheryl also pinned her colours to the Olly mast and said: 'Boys, I have really loved you over the past few weeks and big kisses, but the act I am going to send home is John and Edward.'

Naturally, there were no surprises when Dannii – who had the deciding vote – opted to send John and Edward home. She said: 'I'm going to have to judge it as I've judged it the whole time. On the premise that it's a singing competition, I will have to send home John and Edward.'

The pair were immediately hugged by Olly and all the remaining contestants as their dream run on live TV came to an end. Gracious in defeat, John thanked the fans for keeping them in the show until then and said: 'It's been the greatest experience of my life. We're here every single weekend on live television having the greatest time of our life.'

That night, a host of celebs took to their Twitter pages to talk about John and Edward's exit. Peaches Geldof, a huge fan of the boys who had even visited them backstage in Louis' dressing room, wrote: 'Jedward are out. I am now going to take a week out for mourning. It may be the end, but we witnessed something truly beautiful. I am crying over this. Great.'

TV presenter Phillip Schofield wrote: 'Nice guys but this week they had to go – enough is enough.

'Thing is that Jedward were on the wrong show – they should have been on *Britain's Got Talent*, where we love a good novelty act.'

John and Edward went on to film their last-ever *Xtra Factor* with Holly Willoughby and told her that they hoped either Stacey or Olly would go on to win the final.

The twins collapsed into the arms of their parents John and Susanna after meeting up with them in Louis' dressing room backstage – and their mentor was quick to tell them this wasn't the end, only the beginning. Edward recalls: 'Louis told us that we could be really proud of ourselves and everyone knew who we were and that maybe the show would go back to Ireland because we had gotten so far – that was cool.

'It was the first time in weeks that we didn't have to think about what song we would do on the next show and that was a bit weird. We didn't really know what to do with ourselves that night.'

Louis admitted that he had a feeling that his act's time was coming to an end earlier that week: 'The fact was that the competition was getting extremely serious and I didn't know how long John and Edward could hold it up to Joe McElderry and Olly, and I knew that when it came down to it, there wasn't much time left for them.

'The real problem was that Irish people couldn't vote for them – they could have stayed in longer, if it were not for that. Can you imagine what they could have done if the Irish could vote for them? They seemed unstoppable as it was, without the support of the Irish. They won over people all over the UK and that is a difficult thing to do as more often or not, they will vote for their own because they might know them or know someone who lives near them or something.

'John and Edward had no one over in the UK and there they were, still on stage in Week Seven. They had the time of their lives and I had the best time working with them.'

Backstage, the teenagers were comforted by their fellow contestants and also received a visit from Cheryl Cole and Simon Cowell, who both wished them well.

'Things changed the night that John and Edward left and everyone knew that it wasn't going to be as much fun anymore,' Louis later recalled. 'It all got a hell of a lot more serious from then on. And I know that all of the remaining acts really missed them from the house, too. They were a force to be reckoned with.'

The twins would later learn that they had actually received more public votes than Olly on the night when they were sent home, but Edward was quick to say that they were not going to dwell on that: 'It's nice to know that our fans were still out there voting for us, but we loved Olly and wanted him to go on and win. It was the judges' decision and Olly stayed, and we were really happy for him,' he insisted.

But it wasn't all bad news for Jedward that fateful night – they found out that they had managed to score a No. 1 single with the rest of the finalists for their cover of Michael Jackson's 'You Are Not Alone'. The song went straight in at the top of the singles charts, meaning that either way, John and Edward were leaving the show on a high.

'Everyone was just hugging each other when we found out that we were No. 1,' John says. 'I mean, a couple of months before that we were just messing around singing in our bedroom in Dublin and then we had a No. 1 single with *X Factor* – I don't know if we knew how to, like, take it all in and keep everything in our heads.

'We never even thought that we would be singing a Michael Jackson song, never mind getting to No. 1 with it – it was so cool and everyone was so happy. We loved making the video and everything. It was like we were finally where we were meant to be and all of the hard work was worth it, and the single was for charity so it was great to give something back.'

Back at home in Dublin, close to 1,000 punters turned up at a pub in their home village of Lucan to support the twins. The Lord Lucan had become the unofficial Jedward HQ in Ireland while the boys were on the show. Over 10 TV screens in the bar were all tuned in to watch the live show. From 6pm onwards, since the live shows had begun, hundreds of fans made their way there to watch the lads.

Local girl Tara Murphy turned up every single week to support Jedward. She admitted: 'We are never really going to get tickets to the show so it's great to come here to soak up the atmosphere. We are so proud of them. Everyone would know them from seeing them around and of course they stuck out because they are a gorgeous pair. 'People in Lucan just wanted to do their little bit to support them and let them know we are here.

'It was hard to see them getting booed but they are going to get a huge reception when they come home – all of the kids in the area are just inspired.'

GMTV also sent a camera crew to the pub one morning, where local TV personality Lorraine Keane reported live with some of John and Edward's biggest Irish fans.

But there were tears all round when the boys were booted off the show and Tara admitted: 'It won't be the same now without them – I doubt I'll even watch it any more. John and Edward were the best thing about this year's series by a mile.'

That Monday morning, the lads were still in shock at having to leave the show – mixed with the high of their first No. 1 single.

But there was to be no rest for John or Edward as they

had to get up at the crack of dawn for their first TV appearance since getting the boot. Each week, the evicted finalists would give their first interview to GMTV on ITV. Wearing white shirts and leather waistcoats, the twins told the nation their secret to staying on the show so long was that they stayed positive.

John revealed: 'I feel that me and Edward didn't really focus on the negative. It's all about being positive and we focus on the people who were kind to us. Everyone on the show was so helpful and helped us in different ways that only we will ever know.'

Edward added: 'Everyone we worked with – Brian Friedman came up with these amazing productions for us; Evie – our vocal coach – also helped us on the show and we are not just representing ourselves, we were representing them because they put so much work into us.'

Asked if they felt that it was their time to leave, John shrugged: 'I feel that every single week, me and Edward worked really hard and stayed up so late every night…'

Edward intervened: 'We always had a general interest in music and we felt that this would be a good way of getting out and doing something cool. We always had a drive to do something.'

On leaving the ITV studios that morning, the twins were to get a feeling of what life for them was now going to be like. Fans were waiting to catch a glimpse of the new celebs while paparazzi fought to get the best picture. They may have been booted off the show in Week Seven, but John and Edward were beginning to get the feeling that things were just starting out for them.

'I think that me and Edward didn't really have that much time to be sad when we left the show because we were so busy the very next day. We didn't really have time to think,' John says. 'You know, one minute we were on the show and the next we were having our last time in the house and saying goodbye to everyone but it was cool because everyone had to go home at some stage. We knew that we were going to see everybody again soon.'

And Edward admits they were both exhausted after nearly two months of preparing for two live shows every weekend: 'When we used to watch *X Factor* at home, we would be dancing around and thinking that it looked like so much fun. It was so much fun, but I don't think anyone knows how long you have to, like, work at just one routine. You could have to do it 20 times a day and still not get it right. And then we would go back to the house and stay up most of the night in our bedroom, like practising – it wasn't a joke and we had to get it right, and sometimes John would tell me to stop messing because he is a little bit more serious. I would always make him laugh in the end, though.'

Later that Monday, John and Edward learned that they were being used in an ad campaign for the General Election in the UK. The Conservative Party had jumped on the Jedward bandwagon and rapidly launched a new poster campaign. The poster featured a bequiffed Gordon Brown and Alistair Darling with the slogan: 'Jedward are gone, but we've still got Deadwood'.

Earlier in the series, Labour had put out a poster featuring Cameron, with the legend: 'You won't be laughing if they win.'

John and Edward were thrilled to learn that they had come to the attention of the politicians in the UK. Prime Minister Gordon Brown had said he thought the twins were 'not very good' while David Cameron admitted he found them addictive.

'It just proved that we had everybody talking, even like the rulers of the country in England,' Edward shrugs. 'We didn't think that they would be watching in, but they looked cool with our hair. Maybe everyone will try to have our hair now, like it was back when The Beatles were around and everyone wanted to look like them.

'Politicians in Ireland might want to grow their hair like John and Edward now – that would be pretty cool.'

Conservative leader David Cameron admitted he regularly tuned into the show and watched John and Edward's performances: 'You only need to watch a few minutes and suddenly, 40 minutes later, you're still nailed to your chair, waiting for the terrible twins to appear.'

One thing was for sure: John and Edward were being talked about in every house in Britain and the UK, and if they wanted a career in showbiz, there was now some serious money to be made.

If the pair had thought for a moment that they were in for a holiday when their stint on the show ended, they were in for a shock. Already they were block-booked well into 2010 and would also be taking part in the *X Factor Live* tour with the rest of the finalists in March and April.

John and Edward took some time to sit down with parents John and Susanna to decide what they were going to do. The boys were still enrolled in Sixth Year back in

Dublin and due to sit the all-important Leaving Certificate in just six months. While Susanna was keen for them to consider returning to school, the reality was that their hectic schedule left little time for study. The Leaving Certificate would have to be put on the back burner as 2010 was shaping up to be the biggest year of their lives.

Both the boys told their parents that they were living the dream and wanted to make the most of it, and that they could always return to school the next year to do their exams. Teacher Susanna was obviously keen to see her sons finish their education so that they would always have something to fall back on, but her baby boys had caught the showbiz bug and were holding on to their newfound fame with a tight grip.

During their first week of freedom from the live shows, Jedward barely had a moment to themselves and were escorted from appearance to appearance – followed everywhere by their legions of fans. John and Edward knew they had built up a large fan base during their time on the show but were still overwhelmed by the reaction they received when back in the real world. Thousands of besotted girls were following their every move, with many breaking down in tears at the mere sight of their now trademark and ever-growing hairstyles.

And the boys were keen that they should give their fans as much time as possible: 'I don't get all these famous people who aren't nice to their fans and run away from them and things,' John says. 'With me and Edward it was never going to be like that: when we see our fans we want to hug them and talk to them, and sign whatever they want and do pictures.

'A couple of weeks after the show we noticed that some of the same girls were everywhere and got to know their names – it's cool. It's like they are your friends when you are away from home. We would never be rude to fans.'

Another benefit that the twins soon discovered to having hoards of followers was that they hardly ever had to put their hands in their pockets. Edward laughed: 'These fans would just turn up with everything for us. Like, they might have heard somewhere that we like fruit, and then we would meet them and they would have apples and oranges for us. Some of them brought us clothes – it was like we didn't need money anymore because fans were bringing us all of these treats.'

After years of looking at their favourite stars like Backstreet Boys and Britney, and wishing they could have lives like them, John and Edward had suddenly achieved the impossible. They were famous beyond even their own expectations – everyone knew their name and they were in hot demand in the UK and Ireland.

Such fame could come as a shock to most people, but the twins said they were ready for it. 'Maybe it was because we thought about it for so long or already knew what our autographs were like or something, but we didn't get a really big fright when people started knowing our names,' Edward said. 'We loved it – we would go to the supermarket and people would be chasing us around. Like, I don't get why people give out about that stuff – it's fun. We would never pass by a fan and like, not talk to them because that's just not nice.'

John chipped in: 'I think that we can be like, the nicest people to our fans in the world. If we were known for that, that would be cool. We want all of our fans to stay with us forever. There are still Beatles fans everywhere and we want Jedward fans to be all over the place years from now.

'It doesn't have to be something that's just for now – if you are nice to people and don't get rude then it can last, I think. Big stars shouldn't be rude and most of the ones we have met are nice – and that's what we are going to keep on doing.'

One of the highlights of their journey so far came when John and Edward received a call they had been waiting on for a long time. It was from a TV station in Ireland, who wanted them as soon as they were off the ITV show.

The Late Late Toy Show is an institution in Ireland and it's the dream of every little boy and girl in the country to appear on it. For years, John and Edward had sat excitedly in their PJs watching the show in the build-up to Christmas every year and dreamed of being on it.

Following their *X Factor* success, the producers were on the phone straightaway. The boys were beyond excited: it was one thing to be going on huge TV shows in the UK but *The Late Late Toy Show* in Ireland? It didn't get any bigger than that.

At the end of the week they would be flying back home for the first time since leaving the show and although they knew that their star had risen in Ireland, the boys were in for a shock. Jedmania had spread far and wide: for them, home would not be the same for a long, long time.

During their last week in the *X Factor* house, John and

Edward were also thrilled to learn that they had been immortalised in a computer game. The free Internet programme drew thousands of hits from fans looking to play the very first Jedward computer game. Players had to keep John and Edward balanced on a seesaw, then bounce them on it in an attempt to grab votes on stage. If the player lost control, then John and Edward got injured and were eventually booted off the show.

The hilarious online game showed computer versions of Jedward calling out 'We won't let you down, Louis!' as they leapt about. If the gamer lost, then a smug computerised version of Simon Cowell appeared with a speech bubble, saying: 'Take them outside… und shute zem!'

Meanwhile, the game page declared: 'Jedward are facing the ultimate humiliation – being voted off *X Factor* 2009. Guide Louis Walsh's pet chipmunks to victory or leave them crashing to the floor or impaled on spikes – like Simon Cowell wants.'

Top software firms then got in touch with *X Factor* bosses to talk about making a money-spinning Jedward game for sale in the shops. One industry expert said in November 2009: 'There has been a lot of talk of an official game starring the twins. They have so many catchphrases and actions – it would make an ideal game.'

WHAT THE JUDGES HAVE TO SAY NOW

Ask Louis Walsh to define what *The X Factor* is and more times than not, the pop maestro will reference Jedward. Louis has been responsible for 70 million record sales across the world, with acts like Westlife, Boyzone,

Samantha Mumba and Shayne Ward all under his wing at one stage.

And as talented as all of his acts are, Louis knew there was something special about John and Edward from the minute he laid eyes on them. 'They already looked like pop stars,' he admits. 'All of the groundwork was done – they just needed a bit of tweaking. I knew that girls were going to love them. They made me laugh at that first audition and they made all of the other judges laugh, too. Everyone was talking about them from day one – and that's when you know that you have something special on your hands.'

Louis didn't debate for too long before deciding to manage John and Edward after their *X Factor* contract had expired. He knew from earlier on in the show that he wanted them on his books, but just didn't know if he would have the time.

'I wanted to be sure that I could give them all the help that they needed and that I would have enough time to do that,' he said. 'Things were hectic with Westlife and the new girl band, and I wondered if John and Edward would be able to fit in with all of that – but they were, and it has all worked out really well.'

While the other judges raised eyebrows when he selected them for the finals of the show, Louis says he always knew what he was doing: 'Listen, I have been in this industry all of my life – I know what is going to work when I see it. I didn't care what the rest of them had to say – none of them could now say a bad word about the twins because they showed them every single week how entertaining they were.

'Simon, Cheryl and Dannii know how successful they have become – they read the papers, they heard about the reception for them on the *X Factor* tour. No one can deny that they were the biggest thing to come out of *X Factor* 2010, and no matter what Simon said to them at the time, he loved having John and Edward around – they made him smile all of the time.'

And Louis is hoping he can find 'another Jedward' in the 2010 series of the show and stir up still more controversy on *The X Factor*: 'It's all about having something different – you don't have to be the most amazing singers in the world to make it in this industry. It's as much about the likeability factor than anything else.

'Even though John and Edward initially came across as cocky, I think that people saw after a while that they were just young kids trying to live a dream and couldn't but like them. The most fun I've ever had backstage was this year with the boys. Everyone who came to the show wanted to meet them and wanted to get their pictures taken with them, from Peaches Geldof to the Black Eyed Peas. They were the real winners and that's why I wanted to manage them.'

After getting them on his books, Walsh appointed former Six singer Liam McKenna as their road manager and immediately began work to launch a nationwide tour of Ireland: 'You have to work fast with acts when *The X Factor* ends because that's when the demand is there. I wanted John and Edward to go all around Ireland to play for their fans, like Boyzone and Westlife used to do – that is where you get the lifelong fans.

'I'm from the country and I know that people love to go to a local theatre to see their favourite acts – everything shouldn't be in Dublin. I was right: 30,000 people snapped up the tickets for Jedward – I was wondering if we should have put them on in Croke Park by themselves because they probably would have sold that out, too,' he laughs.

'Touring is so important and John and Edward couldn't wait to get on the road – they had the time of their lives and their parents were able to join them whenever they could. I made sure that they were well looked after, and they aren't even into pubs and partying so there were no worries there – all that they wanted to do is get onto the stage and sing.'

Louis admits that his time managing Jedward has been one of the most hectic duties of his career: 'Their schedule would just make your eyes water and they never once complain; that is why I said months ago that they were going to be millionaires and that is why they are – John and Edward just love what they do and more than anything, they love getting out there to meet all of the fans. Their fans mean everything to them and in return for the love they show them, the fans give it back.'

Walsh and Jedward have had the last laugh after months of torment from naysayers and haters while they were on *The X Factor*. And Louis reckons that the show will go on for a long time to come: 'These boys can turn their hands to anything – they are incredible. I still think that they will be brilliant TV presenters. I also think that Americans would love them and they could be superstars over there. The world is their oyster.

'Disney would be perfect for them – or they could go full-time as models. Listen, they can do anything that they want in the world! Everybody loves them.'

Simon Cowell is the first to admit that he never thought Jedward would cause such a stir on the show. Also, he didn't think that a year later they would be the proud owners of a No. 1 single and album.

'I'm honestly happy for the boys – they are having an incredible journey,' he says. 'You know, they are what the show is all about – making these dreams come true. While they didn't win – even though I was beginning to worry that they would at one stage – Jedward have gone on to achieve a lot and they are still around. Who can argue with that?'

While the show's boss always states he is looking for singing sensations that can be known all around the world, he loves to watch what he dubbed 'the novelty acts' coming up through the ranks: 'With John and Edward, we just didn't know what they were going to come out with from one end of the week until the next and yes, that made it bloody exciting to watch – even if it was through your hands most of the time! They entertained.'

And one thing that Cowell believes will always stand the twins in good stead was how they conducted themselves while being booed on stage and targeted by online hate sites.

'I don't think that we ever had an act that caused a reaction like that before on the show and those boys never once let it show. Each week they came back fighting and that really showed me how strong they both are. That has stood to them and is why they are still here while the new series is preparing to kick off: they get down, they are what they are and they don't apologise for it – I have to admire them for that.'

Cheryl Cole admits to having a soft spot for the twins soon after meeting them for the very first time: 'I think at first, when they came out on stage for that very first audition, we thought they were just so full of themselves. But after a few moments you couldn't help but smile – they just put you in a good mood from day one.'

Kind-hearted Chezza frequently gave the twins positive feedback and felt a sort of motherly instinct towards them while they were on the show: 'John and Edward had such a tough ride – they were so young and I just don't know where they found the strength to come out every week and smile. I think that is what made people just fall in love with them – they triumphed above everything that was thrown at them, they showed just how strong they are.'

While no one envisaged that John and Edward would survive until Week Seven of the live shows, Cheryl is not surprised that they are still on the scene: 'I think that young kids just love them and they have since they first came on the show. I'm happy that they are doing so well for themselves – they were always so nice and polite and brought a smile to my face. I used to look forward to seeing them every week and things seemed to get far more serious on the show as soon as they were gone, I think.'

Aussie judge Dannii Minogue was probably the second harshest critic of John and Edward – after Simon Cowell. Dannii famously saw red when her act Lucie Jones got the boot and the twins remained on in the show, but shrugs:

'That's showbiz, I suppose. Whatever you say, 2009 was a year that John and Edward just seemed to take over. People just lapped them up and it was terrific for the show. You never knew what they were going to come out with, yet they tried so hard to entertain us all.

'They did entertain us all – but I think that when they did leave the show, the time was right as it was a singing competition and there were far stronger singers.'

But even Dannii has to admit that the cheeky duo made her laugh: 'I know that all of the other contestants in 2009 really missed them when they were gone out of the house because they were always fooling around. While we all wondered what Louis Walsh was doing by selecting them for his final acts, he seems to have shown each one of us that he knew what he was doing. Louis saw something there from day one and we all wish them every success, of course.'

chapter seven

after X factor

THE TWINS CAUSED absolute pandemonium when they turned up at RTE studios in Dublin for their appearance on *The Late Late Toy Show* just one week after getting the boot from *The X Factor*.

This was no ordinary television appearance. *The Late Late Show* is Ireland's number one chat show and the *Toy Show* attracts the largest audience figures out of any TV show in the country.

Hours before the programme was scheduled to begin recording security began to place barriers around the large city centre campus in Dublin. Eager fans had already begun to gather – but these were not *Toy-Show* fans, these were Jedward fans. Never before had the station bosses been forced to go to such lengths to keep fans at bay. Jedwardmania had hit Dublin. Schoolgirls from all over the country spent hours waiting in the freezing cold for their heroes to arrive. And when John and Edward got to

RTE, they went against the advice of their minders and ran straight for their legions of adoring fans.

'This is one of the best days so far – we never dreamed that we would be on *The Toy Show*,' said Edward. 'We always watched it when we were younger and wished that we could get on there and play. Then we arrived at the studio and there were all these fans outside screaming our names – we couldn't believe it. Security wanted us to go inside, but we just had to see them all and say hi.'

After meeting with their Jedmaniacs, the lads prepared for their début on the show with host Ryan Tubridy. And even though 'Tubs' can be a pretty serious presenter, Jedward wasted no time in making him laugh by attacking him live onset in a bid to give him a matching hairdo.

Audience figures for the show on 27 November 2009 were the highest in Ireland for years. Many say this was in no small part down to the appearance from the twins. After making a grand entrance through the audience, the boys came face to face with their long-lost older triplet in the form of presenter Ryan. Wearing shiny bronze suits, Jedward sang and danced their way through the delighted audience before back-flipping their way onto the set.

'We are so excited to be here,' they said in unison, before John added, 'Christmas wasn't Christmas without this, so this is a real highlight for us tonight.'

Tubridy was equally pleased to have them on the show: 'We have been going through such hard times and Jedward distracted us and they did so really well. They're wonderfully ridiculous and they know that.'

Next up for the lads was a return trip to the UK with even

hn and Edward have loved running since they were young lads so launching
e Great Ireland Run was the perfect job for them.

Author Jennifer O'Brien with the boys.

edward in La La Land. The boys have fun on a Stateside visit.

Jedmania! The crowds turn out to the launch of the boys' single, *Under Pressur*

Opposite, *below*: John and Edward with their mini counterparts.

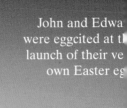

John and Edwa
were eggcited at t
launch of their ve
own Easter eg

h yes they did! John and Edward get set for the pantomime season.

Above: Jedward with legendary rapper Vanilla Ice. The three are now good friends and Vanilla Ice even admitted he was thinking of getting a Jedward tattoo!

Below: John and Edward thought it was cool to be invited on the last ever series of *Big Brother*.

more TV appearances. They got the surprise of their lives to open up the paper on 1 December and learn that they were being tipped for an appearance on their favourite show – *The Simpsons*. And yes, when contacted by the *Irish Sun*, a producer for Fox, who make the show, confirmed that they were 'taking a look at the boys.'

He said: 'Here at *The Simpsons* we love anything Irish – we set a whole show there last year. Jedward certainly are charming and good-looking fellows.'

The lads were high as kites on learning that they might join the likes of Bono, Simon Cowell and Susan Boyle in getting a cameo role on their favourite TV show. Edward admitted: 'This is the coolest thing ever. I can't believe that they even know who we are! I'd love if we could get on and be like best friends with Bart or something like that. He is always messing like us – I think Jedward and Bart could really be good friends.'

As *The X Factor* final in the UK drew close, the boys prepared for a return to the studio where it all began to meet up with their friends from the show. Judge Louis tipped Joe McElderry to win the crown, but said he believed that Jedward were the *real* winners of the show.

Walsh, who decided to take the boys under his wing after they got the boot, reckoned that he knew a good pair when he saw them. 'There has never been anything like them and I am so excited to be managing them,' he declared. 'John and Edward are two of the nicest guys that I have ever met. I always knew that there was something special about them, but I didn't pick them because they were Irish – I picked them because they were so special.'

He then showed why he is one of the most successful band managers in the world by predicting a huge year for Jedward in 2010. And even though nasty Simon was constantly giving the boys a tough time and scoffed at his decision to manage the boys, Louis insisted John and Edward would have the last laugh.

'I think that 2010 could be *the* year of Jedward,' he pronounced. 'I just think that they are going to take off and have the biggest year of their lives. *The X Factor* is only the beginning for them – John and Edward are much bigger than *The X Factor*!'

Indeed, it turned out that Walsh, as usual, had his finger right on the pulse and 2010 would be 'The Year of the Jed'.

After months on the show and many ups and downs the boys were thrilled to get a couple of days off to head back to their family home for Christmas. But it was back to work on St Stephen's Day (Boxing Day) as they turned up to cut the ribbon at the opening of department store Arnotts in Dublin City Centre.

'We got one day off and we just slept,' said John after Christmas. 'It was a nice Christmas, though – with our family and our pets – and we were just back to being normal.' Edward chipped in: 'When you go in the door at home and your mom is there making dinner, it's like time has just frozen – everything is just the same. I love that about going home.

'We slept and opened presents, and compared our new runners but then we wanted to get back out there and see our fans again.'

The boys once again drew record crowds for the opening

of the Winter Sales before heading back to the UK for some New Year's TV appearances. By now, Louis and the team had a day-by-day jam-packed schedule that would take John and Edward right through till the end of 2010.

Offers of gigs, TV appearances, personal appearances and product endorsement had been flooding in from Ireland, the UK and some of Mainland Europe. Everyone wanted a piece of the boys, and everything that they put their hand to, it seemed, turned to gold.

One PR expert admitted: 'From the time the boys left *The X Factor* they were the biggest endorsement that you could get. The best thing about them is that they know exactly what photographers want – they were born to be in front of the cameras and their shots always land in the papers.'

The expert added: 'What is unusual about them is that they transcend genres. Broadsheet newspapers seem to love them just as much as the tabloids. If you had enough money in 2010 then John and Edward were the people you wanted to get on board.'

The twins were thrilled when chat-show host Graham Norton said he wanted them on his New Year's Eve show for the BBC. And when Jedward arrived at the studio in London, they got a huge surprise when they heard that *Sex and the City* star Sarah Jessica Parker would be sitting on the couch beside them during the show. SJP was instantly smitten and told Graham Norton: 'Gosh, they are so lovely!'

When describing the twins to SJP, Norton told her: 'The thing about them is, they are boys with high hair, who like jumping around the place, having a bit of a sing.' US chat-show host Joan Rivers was also on the panel and shook her head in astonishment at the sight of the Dublin boys.

When Cork native Norton described them as 'posh Irish', John and Edward were quick to tell him otherwise. 'We're not posh,' they insisted in unison.

'Our friends go clubbing and drinking and smoking, and that kind of thing but we never do any of that. We are going to go see a movie or something, we are always running and doing sports, and are just really focussed on what we are doing.'

The boys' funny interview went on to get over 80,000 hits on YouTube as well as attracting millions of viewers on the night it was broadcast. And they admitted having to pinch themselves when they sat down beside SJP.

'We just kept looking at her and it was like, oh my god, it's Sarah Jessica Parker!' said John. 'She has twins too, so we were asking her all about them and telling her how cool it is to be a twin. We loved it, and Graham is always really nice to us and he's Irish too, so that's fun.

'He really makes us laugh and it's such a fun show. I mean, if Sarah Jessica Parker and Joan Rivers are on, well, that means that it's a pretty big deal so we were happy to do the New Year's Eve show.'

chapter eight

preparing for take-off and into 2010

THE TWINS ENTERED 2010 with a determination to become bigger and more successful than ever before. They were truly focussed on keeping their place in the limelight and determined not to let all their hard work go to waste.

As far as John and Edward were concerned, they hadn't sat through weeks of abuse from audience members on *The X Factor* for nothing – they had managed to build up an even thicker skin. While 9 out of 10 reality show contestants disappear down the deep black hole of washed-up wannabes when the show ends, the Grimes brothers were committed to sticking around. The duo were just warming up for world domination.

Since the sixth series of *X Factor* had wrapped, they were without a doubt the most talked-about stars of the show. While likeable Stacey Solomon and Olly Murs were still attracting some media attention and winner Joe McElderry was celebrating his victory, Jedward were hogging more limelight than any of them put together. Yards of newspaper columns in Ireland and Britain were dedicated to the new phenomenon that was sweeping the world of celebrity. Some loved to loathe them, still more were loathe to love them – either way, the boys were everywhere and as they say: 'The only thing worse than being talked about is *not* being talked about.'

The twins were even given the honour of guest editing Gordon Smart's 'Bizarre' column in the *Sun* – a feat only been achieved by a handful of stars. John and Edward were quick out of the traps in 2010 and wasted no time in telling the public that they weren't going to be going anywhere that year.

John said sternly: 'Me and Edward are going to show that we are not some flash-in the-pan act. We are not a novelty and are going to stick around. We won't stop until we are top of the charts, and even then we will keep going.'

Those determined comments from the younger twin indicate the lads are also into the business side of things. While many would be of the opinion that Jedward are just enjoying the ride and going with the flow, those who have met them frequently can see that the boys know exactly how to 'work it'. Far from being naïve or deluded, the twins knew what they wanted and they went out and got it, taking no prisoners along the way.

Their hunger for success was something that Louis Walsh saw in them from the very first day. 'I knew that they seemed a lot younger than 17, but I quickly learned that these guys had serious ambition,' he says. 'They have their heads screwed on. They don't drink, they don't do drugs – they are the healthiest pair of kids that you have ever laid your eyes on. They never complain and they just want to work, work, work – how would I ever regret taking them on?

'The boys are a manager's dream and they are having the time of their lives. They work it with everything they have. People laughed at them, but they are incredible: they have an incredible memory, they meet people and always remember them and in showbiz that is vital. They know exactly what to do and people gravitate towards them in a room. Jedward has the X factor and that's what the show is all about. They weren't the best singers by a long shot, but by God, they were the best entertainers!'

As the lads' fame grew, they took to online networking site Twitter to keep in touch with their fan base. And under the name Planet Jedward, they were soon well on the way to attracting 50,000 followers, who were hanging on to their every Tweet. The clever pair also began to follow huge celebs throughout the world and send them amusing messages. Soon it emerged that Edward was developing a bit of an online crush on American country singer Taylor Swift. The smitten star began to send her online messages with romantic lyrics from her own songs in January 2010. He wrote: 'Take me somewhere we can be alone. You'll be the Princess and I'll be the Prince. It's a love story, baby, just say yes.'

But Jedward's legion of female followers soon became jealous and began to bombard Swift's site with messages telling her to leave the twins alone. John admitted: 'That was kind of embarrassing because we were the ones who were sending her messages. It was funny, though. We have lots of girlfriends and we don't just want one. Edward likes Taylor's songs.

'Me and Edward would never fall out over a girl – no way. And we would never want to fall out with our fans over a girl, either.'

The boys began to successfully use Twitter to drum up support for their upcoming single releases and by constantly posting messages and pictures online for fans to see, they ensured that they were always being talked about. It wasn't long before the pair decided to branch out into their own TV station and so they set up Jedward TV on YouTube to keep their adoring fans up to date with their every move.

'Jedettes' who were following the lads on Twitter soon joined up with the TV channel and the lads frequently updated video diaries, including one of them pretending to fly a plane!

Most of January was spent in the UK as the lads lined up TV deals and did countless interviews. On 9 January, they learned that they would be performing at the National Television Awards in Britain in front of some of the biggest names in showbiz in the UK. Better still, all of the old *X Factor* judges were set to be in attendance but they were the only ones from the show who would be performing.

The twins were determined to keep details of their big performance under wraps and all the show's producers would say was that the stage would be decorated with thousands of Swarovski crystals for their performance. But behind the scenes, John and Edward were holding on tight to a massive secret: record company execs had managed to line up legendary 90's rapper Vanilla Ice to duet with them on his hit single 'Ice Ice Baby'.

Management didn't tell the twins the news until the very last minute for fear the chatty pair would let the cat out of the bag. However, the media soon learned of their upcoming duet and the lads hit the front pages in Ireland.

Vanilla Ice, whose real name is Robert Matthew Van Winkle, jumped at the chance to team up with Jedward in the hope of reigniting his career. And Louis was only too happy to get him on-board. At the time Walsh admitted: 'The boys are beyond excited about working with Vanilla Ice – I have never seen them so excited. This song is going to be a hit. There is going to be a mix with Queen also – it's funky.'

Jedward finally got to meet with Vanilla Ice just days before the TV Awards to work on their routine. The rapper was flown in from LA by execs at Sony, who were determined to make Jedward's first single a No. 1 hit. If the twins were going to have a successful music career ahead of them, the live TV performance of the single was vital.

And so the lads spent hours in rehearsals with Vanilla, who immediately took them under his wing. The threesome spent a weekend locked away in a London recording studio laying down the music for their first-ever single release. And Vanilla Ice himself was soon taken with John and Edward. He admitted: 'I just fell in love with them – they were like little balls of energy from the moment that we met. I hadn't heard of them before this offer, but I'm extremely excited about it. Kids love them and it's a chance to bring my music to a much younger audience. Hell, they even look like me when I was younger – it's perfect!'

Indeed, it was perfect. The lads wowed the audience including Simon, Cheryl and Dannii when they took to the stage at London's O2 Arena on 20 January. Celebrity choreographer Brian Friedman was once again drafted in to work his magic on the boys and 'Ice Ice Baby' stole the show. Simon grinned like a Cheshire cat, while Dannii and Cheryl clapped along to the performance. But most importantly for the record company execs at Sony who were watching, the rest of the audience loved it too.

Louis admitted: 'We knew after those awards that "Ice Ice Baby" could be a big hit. It's catchy, it's funny, it has a guest rapper – how could it fail? It was the perfect first song choice for the boys.'

After their show-stopping performance, the lads prepared for a trip stateside to make the accompanying video with Vanilla Ice. And even though their first single had not been released yet, already they were lining up a wishlist of who they wanted to collaborate with next.

John said: 'We would love to team up with Britney Spears, Taylor Swift or Miley Cyrus. We are just kind of putting the word out there now so that everybody knows that. I mean, stranger things have happened: who would have thought that we would end up writing and doing a video with Vanilla Ice?'

Thousands of fans logged onto the Internet to watch re-runs of their show-stopping NTA performance while management rubbed their hands in glee – there was no doubt that they had a hit on their hands with 'Ice Ice Baby' and it was important to get it on sale as soon as possible.

Across the Atlantic, the boys were also beginning to attract some attention. Teaming up with Vanilla Ice had meant that news of them spread stateside and people began to ask who the quiff-haired duo were and where they had come from. Blogger to the stars Perez Hilton was one of the first to take notice and soon posted a link on his massive website Perezhilton.com.

Hilton had stumbled across their single video with Vanilla Ice and decided to showcase them to his followers. The site which attracts over 10 million hits a day brought John and Edward to a bigger audience than they had ever dreamed possible. And Hilton gave the boys his backing in their bid to take over the music world. He wrote: 'Jedward mania hit the UK while these marginally talented twins competed on *The X Factor*. They may not have won the show but they definitely won in other ways. For example, we have not mentioned the winner of this year's *X Factor* – nor are we posting his song. But we have just mentioned Jedward and now we present "Under Pressure (Ice Ice Baby)", a mash-up of the Queen and Vanilla Ice classics sung by Jedward, featuring a cameo by Vanilla himself. This is pure Velveeta! Enjoy.'

Reviews on the site were overwhelmingly good and the boys were chuffed to come to the attention of such a huge showbiz-gossip star.

The video, which features the boys dancing with Vanilla Ice and a troupe of backing dancers, was complete and set for release for the end of January 2010. Top graffiti artists were drafted in to create the backdrop to the shoot and the twins sharpened their look with tailored suits and aviator sunglasses.

Later that month, Irish radio station Spin 103.8 launched a campaign to get Jedward to appear on the Main Stage at 2010's Oxegen Festival alongside huge stars such as Jay-Z and Eminem. A Facebook page was also set up, where thousands of fans joined the campaign to have the lads perform at Ireland's biggest rock festival and although reports at the time suggested they had been offered a slot, their schedule was in fact already full for July – ruling them out of the performance.

Meanwhile, 'Ice Ice Baby' was topping the Most Requested slots on radio shows all over Ireland and the UK. The single seemed well on its way to the very top of the charts – Jedward were on fire, and no amount of 'Ice Ice Baby' was going to put that fire out.

January ended with a bang as Jedward landed an appearance on *The Jonathan Ross Show* on BBC1. The programme, which for years had been home to Ross's hilarious interviews with A-list celebrities made a clear statement to the public: Jedward were bigger than ever and going nowhere.

The boys had the audience at the BBC studio in stitches with their hyper antics as they worked their charm on presenter Ross. In what was their most hilarious TV appearance to date, John and Edward admitted: 'We love Jonathan Ross and were the only people from the show to get on it before it finished.'

John and Edward had the audience in fits for over 10

minutes with their amusing answers and refusal to stop talking. Indeed, clips from their slot on the show have gained over 75,000 YouTube views to date.

The boys leapt onto the famous couch after a clip of them performing 'Ghostbusters' and John told the presenter: 'I ain't afraid of no Jonathan.' Asked which one was John and which was Edward, the lads confused things by going on to talk about their various scars without actually answering the question. Ross told them: 'I still don't know which is which, all I have now is a series of charming disfigurements!'

In a clever marketing ploy, it was agreed that the exclusive première of their *Ice Ice Baby* video with Vanilla Ice would be shown on the show. And it worked a treat: what better place to launch your video than on one of Britain and Ireland's most-watched chat shows?

Ross was extremely taken by the pair, but joked: 'Please God, tell me there isn't a triplet at home!'

After the recording, which also featured *Sex and the City* star Kim Cattrall, Ross invited Jedward to come onto his radio show and swapped phone numbers with them. He gushed: 'They really have something and are extremely charming – say what you like, they were everything that is good about Saturday-night entertainment!'

And there was more good news in store for the boys when they learned that they would be supporting Westlife at Croke Park in Dublin. The gig, which would be performed in front of an audience of 80,000, would be the lads' biggest concert to date. And both John and Edward were over the moon to be performing with their heroes.

Just a few weeks earlier they had found themselves sitting behind the Westlife boys on a flight home to Dublin. And Jedward could not believe it when Westlife star Nicky Byrne asked for their autograph. Dubliner Nicky, who has twin boys Rocco and Jay, told the twins that his children were obsessed with them and got their picture. John and Edward were overwhelmed that Ireland's most successful boy band had any idea who they were.

'First, we gave Nicky our autograph and now we are going to get to sing at Croke Park,' Edward raved. 'It's just getting better and better – and we just have to pinch ourselves sometimes!'

The dream continued into February when the rising superstars were informed that their début single had gone straight to No. 1 in Ireland. And in typical squeaky-clean style, John and Edward celebrated their victory with a bowl of Frosties. The lads topped off their hectic week with an appearance on RTE One's *The Saturday Night Show* with Brendan O'Connor and told him: 'They are playing our songs in Canada, we are like the new Rolling Stones!'

But with every high, there must come a low and Jedward failed to land the No. 1 spot in the UK charts. What was even more heartbreaking was the fact that they had only missed out by 24 sales to Owl City. A defiant John and Edward vowed to carry on and make it to the top of the charts the next time, but the bosses at Sony were already beginning to reassess whether they would keep Jedward on their books.

Tough times in the music industry meant that few acts

were surviving in 2010. Jedward's failure (if only by 24 sales) to reach the top spot in the UK meant that record company bosses were beginning to think twice about whether they could afford to keep them on.

One company exec revealed: 'If you get to No. 1 in the UK you are laughing, but as with most things, there are no prizes for second best. Sony began to wonder if Jedward were more of a phenomenon in Ireland than anywhere else – cuts were going to have to be made, and they had to decide who with.'

But for now, John and Edward were safe.

February also saw the Class of *X Factor* 2009 reunited for the *X Factor Live* tour of the UK and Ireland. The twins were delighted to be back on the road to perform with all of the pals they had made on the show. Olly Murs was one of the performers they were close to, as well as Stacey Solomon.

The tour kicked off in Liverpool, with nine of the final twelve acts from the show taking to the road for over two months. But trouble soon brewed as reports emerged that some finalists were none too happy with the amount of stage time that the twins were getting.

Jedward managed to get more songs than some of the other performers for the live shows and this sparked off a series of rows and ill feeling on the road. But, as usual, John and Edward refused to let sour grapes get them down and carried on regardless.

John admitted in February: 'We have like, three or four songs and the others have two on the tour. It's because of this year's show and all the stuff there was about us. We aren't going to complain – it's what we are being told to do and we are just going to go out there and do it.'

Edward added: 'It's because we have a single out and everything. We don't pay attention if people are not happy with us: me and John just do our own thing. Don't let the haters get you down.'

At the same time show sources admitted that some of the other performers were miffed at the amount of attention the boys were getting. One told the *Sun*: 'This year has been all about Jedward on the show. Everyone knows that and the contestants themselves all know that. They are worried as their flames seem to be burning less bright and the boys seem to be conquering the world.'

Jedward managed to steal the show on every date with their flying 'Ghostbusters' routine that saw them suspended above the audience in harnesses. The lads also continued their cheeky antics on tour, informing fans of their whereabouts and creating massive security alerts at hotels the length and breadth of the country.

The hectic tour took in a massive 50 dates across the UK and Ireland, but it was the dates at Dublin's O2 in March that really had the boys excited. Jedward were finally coming home for a live performance in front of their Irish fans – these were the dates that they had been waiting for.

'Those were the special ones,' John admitted. 'Our friends and our family were able to come and see us, and we hadn't been home in a long time so our fans in Dublin hadn't got to see us. It was just amazing to be on stage there in the O2 and we liked showing the others around Dublin too.'

Hundreds of X Factor fans gathered outside of the boys' city centre hotel in Dublin from their arrival on 16 March until they left on the 18th. And demand to see Jedward was so high, X Factor bosses added another two dates to the Irish leg of the tour to keep the punters happy.

Tickets for Jedward's first-ever nationwide tour of Ireland went on sale at the end of February. The lads broke records at the box office and managed to sell a whopping 30,000 tickets for dates all around Ireland in a matter of minutes. But because of their time on the road with X Factor, John and Edward had just one week to put their show together for the Irish fans.

John revealed: 'Last year nobody even knew who we are – now we are selling out venues all over Ireland. It's going to be like nothing we have ever done before. All of our Irish fans are going to get the best night out and we are coming to a town near you soon.'

Both admitted that their 50-date X Factor tour had been tiring, but the fans had kept them going. Recalled Edward, 'Most of the people who came to see us on the last tour were not X Factor fans, they were John and Edward fans, and they follow us everywhere. The girls check into the hotels that we are in and sleep in the rooms next to us. We don't think they are weird, we think it's cool! They turn up at breakfast and they ask us to sign plates and pepper shakers; they are like our friends. They follow our mum and aunt around, too.

'They have Jedward tattooed across their chests or on their back. The single cover is the latest tatt to get – it's kind of cool!'

Just before the lads were due to take to the stage with the *X Factor* tour on 16 March, they learned that Sony had let them go after just one single. As papers launched into stories about how this would finish Jedward off, Louis Walsh vowed to get them another deal. He said: 'There was only ever one single deal with Sony – I'm going to make an album with them. There aren't enough days in the year for the amount of work I have lined up for them. They are busier than ever and another major label will take them on board and we are going to make an album.

'They've had a No. 1 single here and have sold 30,000 tickets – they are massive and this means nothing except that we are going elsewhere.'

True to his word, Walsh signed a lucrative multi-million Euro contract with Universal Records the very next day. Clever Louis had brought some top execs from Universal along to see the twins perform at the O2 Arena on 17 March 2010. As usual, John and Edward stole the show and received the loudest cheers from the 14,000 fans who travelled to see them.

Record company bosses were so bowled over by the reaction Jedward got from the audience that they said they wanted to sign them that very night. And it turned out that being released from Sony worked to the boys' advantage: plans were put into action to get them working on their début album as soon as possible.

Jedward got straight to work on their début album immediately after the *X Factor Live* tour finished. It was hectic as usual because the lads had just a couple of weeks before they were due to take to the road again with their very own nationwide tour. Within minutes of tickets going on sale, promoters Aiken reported that all tickets for the 27 dates around Ireland had been sold out!

The tour (from 7 April to 1 May 2010) would take Jedward from Galway to Derry and Killarney, and everywhere in between. Just months after being in *The X Factor*, Jedward had sold over 30,000 tickets for their solo tour.

Sinéad Waters of Aiken Promotions admitted the Jedward tour had been one of the most in-demand gigs they handled in 2010. 'Tickets just flew out the door and our phone lines were jammed the minute that they went on sale,' she revealed. 'Demand was so high that I am sure we could have sold many, many more tickets for Jedward dates, if we had them to sell. They are the hottest tickets around right now.'

The first date of Jedward's 27-date tour was in front of 2,000 fans at the Royal Theatre in Castlebar, County Mayo. Jedward lovers who had not managed to get tickets for the gig waited outside in the hope of catching a glimpse of their heroes. And shortly after 8pm, after having just one week to learn all their moves, John and Edward took to the stage amid deafening screams.

It was the first night of their very own show: it was sold out and the atmosphere was electric.

Of all the groups to make it to *The X Factor* finals, John and Edward were the first to take to the road. Make no bones about it, these boys would not rest on their laurels and were more than keen to make hay while the sun was still shining. Even after a 50-date tour, recording an album and a week of rehearsals, the twins managed to bounce around on stage, much to the delight of their followers.

They played show favourites such as 'Ghostbusters' and a number of new covers like 'Candy' and Blink 182's 'All the Small Things' – hinting at what would later go on to appear on their album. And they drew screams from the audience after slipping into their red Lycra jumpsuits from the show to recreate 'Oops!… I Did It Again' by Britney Spears.

John and Edward were also cheered on by a proud John and Susanna, who travelled to Mayo for the concert: the twins' parents travelled to as many of their nationwide tour dates as they could and spoke with the boys on the phone every day while they were on the road.

Speaking after the first gig, a breathless John said: 'That was the best feeling in the world! They were all here, just for me and Edward – we can't wait for the next one.' And in true showbiz style, they didn't have to. The rest of April was spent touring all over the country to sell-out shows. The boys travelled in a blacked-out van and tried to catch up on their sleep while they were on the road.

Their tour manager, Liam McKenna (who also works on *The X Factor*), admitted: 'They never seem to sleep. I was in my hotel room and you can just hear them singing through the walls. We were in Limerick one night, and they came over and said they wanted to go to Dunnes to get food in the middle of the night. So we went over and all they wanted was fruit and water, and then they were trying to pay for it themselves. I told them: "It's OK, guys – we will look after all that stuff for you." They are really funny and innocent like that.'

McKenna, who was a member of pop group Six, which Louis helped put together, revealed that the twins also love to wind him up: 'I could come out my door and they will be standing there singing the Six song, "A Whole Lot of Loving", and just laughing their heads off. I have never met two people with more energy – the entire time on the road, they just kept going and going.'

And he had the added responsibility of trying to keep the twins out of danger once they got up on stage and admitted that both John and Edward were a tad accident prone: 'They might get on there with shoelaces open or something like that and you just can't relax watching them at all. They jump all around the place and you just never know where they are going to end up. It's a full-time job because you don't want them to hurt themselves and they get so hyper.'

He is baffled by the fact that the boys never eat or drink anything unhealthy, yet they are constantly hyper: 'All they have on the road is fruit and water – I have never seen anything like it. They don't really like sweets or crisps and you would never see them with Red Bull. Both of them have so much energy and are constantly on the move – I suppose it comes from how fit they are from running.'

McKenna also has to be constantly on the lookout for over-eager fans who try to sneak their way into the boys' tour bus or even into their beds. He said: 'Those girls could just do anything: there are some fans who would go to any lengths to meet the boys. We have been chased down motorways by fans in cars and found some of them trying to sneak in around the back door of their hotels. And John and Edward add to it all by telling the world where they are on Twitter and next thing you know, you are surrounded.

'They love every minute of it and I have never seen them be rude to a fan. I have never even heard them curse – I don't think they know any swear words. How two people can spend that much time together I do not know, but it's a laugh a minute on the road.'

On 10 April, the *Irish Sun* got to spend a day with Jedward as they embarked on two solo gigs in Dublin. Here's a glimpse of what it's like to be in the eye of the storm that is Jedmania.

8am: The boys are woken following their show in Limerick on Thursday night and board their bus for Dublin.

11.30am: They arrive at DCU, where they'll perform two sell-out gigs. John reveals: 'We are really excited because our family and friends are coming. We are too excited to be tired!'

12pm: The athletic duo head to the running track to launch the Great Ireland Run and pose for pics with fans. Edward says: 'We love to run, so this is perfect – we could run all day long.'

12.45pm: Jedward leg it to the theatre and change into jeans, shirts and ties.

Preparing For Take-off and Into 2010

1pm: At the fans' 'meet and greet' one teen jumps on John and wraps her legs around him, telling him she loves him. He tells her 'We love you too' and signs her arm. Another girl asks John if he has a girlfriend and he delights her by replying: 'We would love ones from Dublin.'

3pm: There's last-minute panic backstage as John is losing his voice but Edward assures him that he will talk for him instead. The boys then perform for a show-stopping hour and a half in front of thousands of screaming fans.

4pm: Time for a quick nap and shower, and then more autograph-signing and posing for snaps. Edward shrugs: 'We don't get tired once our fans are there,' while Louis remarks: 'I have never seen either of them in a bad mood.'

8pm: Show time once again for another 3,000 screaming fans and the boys do not disappoint.

10pm: A weary John and Edward take to their tour bus for a trip to Derry, where they'll play two more shows tonight. 'Dublin, high five, you have been the best!' they remark to the waiting fans before heading off into the night.

The boys toured around Ireland non-stop for one month and even took time to meet some very special fans along the way. While playing dates in Limerick, they met up with young Gavin and Millie, who were victims of a horrific arson attack in the city. The young brother and sister, who were aged 4 and 6 at the time of the attack, were sitting in their car when a bottle filled with petrol was set alight and thrown through the window. Gavin's left ear was burnt off in the inferno and he suffered burns to 22 per cent of his body. Little Millie suffered third-degree burns to her right arm, right thigh and back, and about 20 per cent of her body. But the brave brother and sister were all smiles when they caught up with Jedward in their home town.

Jedward gave the siblings VIP treatment and met up with them backstage following their gig at the University Concert Hall in Limerick. Afterwards the twins admitted that it had been a special moment in their career. John said: 'I remember seeing Gavin and Millie on TV and I'm delighted that they had fun at our concert – they were really cool and we loved getting to meet up with them. We just hope they had lots and lots of fun.'

As the boys' popularity continued to rise in early 2010, they started to gather a huge number of celebrity fans too. Having won over Beatles' legend Sir Paul McCartney on the show the previous November, the twins by now had lots more famous names to add to their list of admirers.

No one expected the hell-raising Pogues' front man Shane McGowan would be a fan, but he admitted: 'I love Jedward, I think that they are great. They are good entertainment and have so much energy about them. I'd definitely record with them. You've got to admire them because they keep going, even though they were criticised the entire time. I can relate y'know.'

And the legendary singer also sung the praises of the lads' manager Louis Walsh and said he was the best man to look after them: 'I've a lot of respect for Louis and I think that he's brilliant at what he does. There's no better man to be their manager.'

Next to talk about the twins was global teen superstar Justin Bieber. Justin, who has sold millions of records around the world, advised Jedward to take a leaf out of his book and always work hard at what they do. He said: 'I always just worked hard all of the time. There have been times when I have flown every day and it's really exhausting, but John and Edward should just keep going. You have gotta fake a smile sometimes.'

In March 2010, Jedward proved that they were just egg-ceptional by landing a deal to launch their very own Easter eggs. The duo launched the eggs in Dublin and added 'No. 1 Fan' chocolate medals inside them as a special gift for their fans. Over 250,000 eggs were made and shipped out to shops all over Ireland ahead of Easter. A bright package featuring the lads' photos on the front and a cutout card on the back appeared on Ireland's top-selling Easter eggs of that year.

The money continued to flow in when Jedward put their name to the line-up of a Christmas Panto at Dublin's Olympia Theatre for a whopping € 150,000. They also received a fee to appear on *Celebrity Big Brother* but Louis immediately ruled that out and simply stated: 'They just weren't prepared to give us enough money.'

Next up came a TV ad for takeaway chain Abrakebabra in Dublin. The lads filmed the 30-second promo at the Donnybrook outlet of the chain, while hundreds of fans waited outside. The hilarious Wild West style ad took just a couple of hours to complete and Jedward bagged a cool £20,000 each for the job. They might be into healthy eating themselves, but a big pay cheque can be very persuasive!

Abrakebabra became the first Irish company to manage to get the twins to endorse their products and the fast food chain's PR Joanne Byrne admitted that they were thrilled to land a deal with Jedward. 'You couldn't have someone more popular than John and Edward at the moment,' she said. 'They were a dream to work with – extremely professional, and came in and got the job done.'

A few weeks later it emerged that the fast food chain had to order more posters featuring Jedward because smitten fans were tearing them off the walls in the restaurant!

John and Edward then decided to put the freshness back by becoming the new faces of Shake n' Vac and pocketed another hefty sum for their troubles. The original ad featured actress Jenny Logan as a dancing housewife singing 'Do the Shake n' Vac and put the freshness back' as she hoovered. As part of their new deal John and Edward filmed a remake of the ad with Logan.

The remake took place in May 2010 and Jedward entered the recording studio to record another version of the iconic Shake 'n' Vac jingle. And both of them stated they had fond memories of using the product, with Edward revealing: 'When we were younger, we had five dogs and we would let them in the house and it would smell bad, and then we would use Shake n' Vac and it would make the carpet smell nice.

'The ad is one of those really cool moments from TV. We don't take ourselves too seriously: we are young and want to have fun with the ads that we do. We are like Shake n' Vac because there is only one of it and there is only one of Jedward too.'

And while offers to endorse products were flooding their management's offices, it seemed the boys could also make money just from being pretty faces. Since their exit in Week Seven of *The X Factor*, model agents both in Ireland and the UK were keen to get the boys on their books.

With flawless good looks, fit bodies and the added bonus of being two of them, Jedward were perfect model material. Although big name modelling agencies from all over were keen to have them on board, the lads made the decision to go with well-known Next Models in the UK. The camera-friendly pair were signed to do some high-end fashion shoots with the possibility of catwalk work also thrown in.

Within weeks, Jedward were brought to a studio in London with a top photographer to pose for shots for their portfolio. And the twins did not disappoint. A series of close-up and topless shots of the boys showed just how catwalk-ready they were and fashion houses began to sit up and take notice.

The agency even received a call from *Italian Vogue*, who said they were keen to feature Jedward in one of their issues and the boys also posed in fashion shoots for *Grazia* magazine.

A thrilled Louis Walsh admitted in April 2010 that he had had to turn down countless jobs for Jedward because they were simply booked solid for months. He revealed: 'Everyone wanted them, from *Celebrity Big Brother* to huge magazines, and we have just had to turn down so many people. They can't be everywhere so we have to go with the best offers for them and things that are going to stand for John and Edward, long-term. They are now signed to Next Models and this is going to be huge for them. If they weren't pop stars, then they could easily be models – anyone can see that.'

Plans were also underway to take Jedward to Japan, where their management and model agency bosses were convinced they could make the big time. A host of sportswear companies and trainer designers were all eager to get the twins signed up to create collections for them – there was still no stopping the Jedward train.

At the end of April, the twins received some sad news when they learned of the sudden death of the iconic Irish broadcaster Gerry Ryan. Gerry, who died suddenly on 30 April, had been one of Jedward's staunchest supporters and constantly talked about them on his 2FM radio show. Indeed, he was the first broadcaster in Ireland to interview them on air in the early stages of their *X Factor* adventures.

Both John and Edward took to the airwaves excitedly, stating, 'Oh my God, I can't believe that we are talking on the Gerry Ryan show – this is amazing!' Ryan himself admitted that he got a 'great kick' out of Jedward and went on to conduct hilarious interviews with them on many other occasions before his untimely passing.

A spoof section of the programme called 'Knob Nation' which features a comedian mimicking famous Irish peoples voices also featured Jedward as soon as they became well known.

In February 2010, Ryan invited the real John and Edward into the studio to come face to face with Oliver Callan, who was mimicking their voices. The result was a hilarious on-air interview between the real Jedward and the fake Jedward, with Gerry asking fans to phone in and tell him which was which.

After his passing, the boys sent their condolences to his grief-stricken family and John admitted: 'He was one of the greats – it was like he was 2FM and we were always so excited to be on his show. He was really funny and always talked about me and Edward, and we will miss him.'

Jedward then dedicated a live version of 'Ice Ice Baby' to Ryan on their Irish tour on the night he died.

The boys had only a couple of days off during April and May and were looking forward to spending them at home in Lucan with their family. However, they soon found out that they were now so famous that sleeping in their own beds was fast becoming impossible. For months, Susanna had been answering the door to besotted fans eager to catch a glimpse of her sons and while she was always welcoming to callers, the situation became impossible when word got round that Jedward were back at home.

John revealed: 'Our mom used to bring them food and bring some of them inside, and in the beginning that was fine. Then I think that people found out that she was feeding them and really nice or something because then more and more would start calling around. They would start knocking really early in the morning and still be there at night – our mum didn't know what to do so the last time we went home, we stayed in a hotel with our mum and brother Kevin.'

And the twins checked into the hotel using false names to ensure no eager fans would be able to trace them. 'We felt like James Bond or something,' Edward said. 'It was cool – we use the names of characters from Disney, like Mickey and Goofy. And the receptionists are looking at us and thinking, those are not your names – it's so funny!'

At one point, things became so manic outside the twins' detached home that the police had to be called in to move the girls on. One neighbour admitted: 'We are all very proud of the boys and loved all the excitement while the show was going on, but nine months later, there are still girls around the place from morning until night and I don't know how their mother copes.

'They could be out there for hours and hours in the hope that John and Edward will come home and they will finally get to meet them. It's madness, but I suppose that is what used to happen to the Beatles too, back in the 1960s – their homes were under siege.'

And it wasn't just fans in Dublin who were getting out of control. A group of girls known as the Jedettes had been following Jedward's every move for months. It didn't help that the lads were experts in whipping their fans into a frenzy: indeed, Edward caused mayhem on the Web by posting a revealing snap of himself on Twitter.

Over 26,000 followers found themselves hot under the collar when the cheeky duo put up a topless picture on the web – and had fans drooling. One admitted the image had reduced her to tears and wrote: 'I cry when I look at this.' Another said: 'Omg.lush pic.xxx you really shouldn't wind us up like this; fair play. Stunning. Love you.'

Later that month on a second appearance on *The Graham Norton Show* on BBC1, the twins admitted that even though the money was supposed to be rolling in, they didn't really care about it. Proving that fame and fortune had not changed their attitudes, John and Edward insisted their career was still all about the fans and they didn't spend lots of money.

John told the presenter: 'It's not a big deal. At the end of the day, people go, 'yeah, I am paying you'. If we bought a house on our own, it would be really scary. I don't think we need to buy a house because if we want to go to America or Paris, or anywhere around the world, then you have to go back to your house.'

And the lads had their host in stitches when they declared: 'We had a tree house but it was knocked down last year!' Then when Norton asked him if he had a cash card, John said: 'I don't know –it doesn't work!'

But the boys admitted in a later interview the one thing they do like to spend cash on is their trademark winged runners. The pair who became famous for their flashy footwear on *The X Factor* admit there's nothing more they like to buy than a new set of runners. Edward said: 'We don't drink, smoke or drive but we love our runners. We run everywhere – that's the only thing that we ever really want to spend money on.'

During 2010, the twins appeared on all the top TV shows in Ireland and the UK. Bosses at television stations were queuing up to have them on – Jedward, as always, were pure TV gold. As well as *The Late Late Show, Jonathan Ross* and *Graham Norton,* John and Edward were interviewed for *GMTV, Loose Women* and *The Saturday Night Show,* to name but a few. Indeed, funny man Graham Norton was so taken with Jedward that he invited them back onto his show in May.

At the end of the month, Jedward flew home to perform at the TV Now Awards at the Mansion House in Dublin. And even though a host of big-name stars from the world of TV in both Ireland and the UK had flown in for the glitzy event, it was once again the John and Edward show.

Hundreds of fans began gathering outside the Mansion House in Dublin City Centre from early evening in anticipation. And shortly after 6pm Jedward arrived and outshone every other star who had turned up for the event.

Corrie legend Bill Roache (Ken Barlow) who was receiving a Lifetime Achievement Award on the night even asked the twins for a snap on the red carpet. And although every journalist and radio station in the country was waiting to interview them, the boys spent more than half an hour meeting with fans and getting their pictures taken with them.

Later that night, Jedward performed live on stage and were watched by manager Louis Walsh, who admitted:

'Things just keep getting better and better! I can't stop the work coming in for these guys. And they are already so professional – they come in, do the work and head off home. I wish every act was like that and then there would be no trouble: Jedward are the best-behaved group I have ever came across in 30 years in the business. They just want to get out there and meet the fans.'

And in true Cinderella style, the lads were smuggled out of the venue straight after their performance and brought back to their hotel. 'They would never stay for an after-party,' Louis admitted, 'It's just not their style at all.' Louis also revealed that he thought Jedward should have been Ireland's entry for the 2010 Eurovision Song Contest.

'I think that they have a very European look and would have been as good as what we did send over,' he said. 'People would have voted for them just for the novelty factor, but it doesn't matter because they wouldn't have had the time to do it even if they wanted to.'

That week the boys also managed to fit in an entertaining interview with TV3's Colette Fitzpatrick on her *Midweek* show, where they revealed that they had lost Victoria Beckham's mobile phone number. John revealed that Posh was a big fan of theirs. He added: 'We BlackBerry messaged her, but we lost it so we don't have anyone's number any more. So all those celebrities are safe knowing that we aren't going to ring them!'

And Edward went on to admit that the pair might consider dating one of their fans in future. He said: 'I think we would because Kevin Jonas from the Jonas Brothers went out with a fan and now he has married her. In a way they are interested in you so that you could be their girlfriend. I think we have thousands of girlfriends.'

In an interview given the previous summer, both the twins admitted they were still virgins and that neither of them had ever had a serious girlfriend. Despite women throwing themselves at them, John and Edward revealed that they simply don't have the time to settle down with any one girl while their careers are taking off.

John said: 'Neither of us has had a serious girlfriend ever: we are virgins. There are lots of girls that come up to me and Edward, but you know, we just don't want one girl. She would have to be very special to be a girlfriend – we just like to be single and just get to know everyone. All of our fans are really friendly and we hug them all.

'We are only 18 and don't have time for girlfriends now – we are never in one place for too long.'

But the lads have never been short of admirers and it didn't take long for some famous faces to notice their model good looks. 'We like Taylor Swift and Britney, and Keisha said that she would like to make out with both of us at once – that might be cool!' John revealed. 'We haven't kissed anyone famous yet, though.'

The start of June 2010 came with the announcement that John and Edward would be releasing 'All The Small Things' by Blink 182 as their second solo single. The pop punk monster, which had been a hit back in 2000, was one of the best received songs that the lads had performed on their recent tour.

And Jedward also revealed that their début album would be called *Planet Jedward*. The boys spent a number of days in a London studio putting their songs together and they were thrilled with their Blink 182 cover.

Edward wrote: 'In the studio and "All The Small Things" is such a rock pop song! We were recording it and we were rocking out and John punched me in the face.'

chapter nine

and so the story continues...

ONE OF THE biggest nights of Jedward's career so far was 5 June, as they prepared to support Westlife at Croke Park, Dublin in front of 80,000 people. Up until that date, the largest group that the twins had performed to was less than 20,000 (not counting the 15 million who used to tune in to watch them on *The X Factor*).

Backstage, the twins were feeling the nerves. John admitted: 'We just don't want to fall over or fall off the stage, or anything like that. There are going to be more eyes on us than ever before. We used to come to Croke Park to watch games and now we are going to be out there singing. We never really get nervous but I think this time we are a bit.'

Jedward were accompanied by their trusty dance troupe from the nationwide tour, and took to the stage that evening in flashy silver jackets 'I love Jedward' and 'Marry

Me, Jedward' posters were visible in the crowd, even though it was a Westlife gig.

John and Edward put in the performance of their lives. Watched once again by Louis Walsh and a host of showbiz hacks from the side of the stage, the lads proved to be the ultimate warm-up act with their high-energy set. Their dance moves were far more polished than on the recent tour and they sailed through five songs without error.

As they ran off stage to huge applause from all the crew, Edward's hand was pumping blood from some high-flying dance manoeuvre, but he smiled through the pain.

Earlier that evening, Shane, Kian, Nicky and Mark from Westlife had stopped by the twins' dressing room to give them some tips on playing in front of 80,000 fans. Edward admitted: 'It was so cool because like, we grew up listening to these boy bands like Backstreet Boys and Westlife and stuff, and now we get to support them. They are always really nice to us, and give us advice and ask if we are feeling OK – it's cool.'

And while superstars Westlife had a long list of backstage demands ahead of their massive performance, Jedward kept it simple. 'We don't really ask for anything,' John insisted. 'All that we want is fruit and water and maybe a bowl of cereal. We don't make a fuss; sometimes the people around us do but we are never really out there, asking for things.

'Westlife are superstars and can ask for whatever they want and they will get it. We might get things too but we don't want everyone running around after us – we are OK and don't need much to make us happy.'

and so the story continues...

June also saw the return of *The X Factor* auditions to Dublin and Jedward could hardly believe it was nearly a year since their lives had changed forever. As Louis, Cheryl, Simon and guest judge Katy Perry prepared to come to Ireland, the lads were urging Irish people to go along to the auditions.

John admitted: 'It's crazy that this time last year no one knew who we were and we were in school and just daydreaming about having our own song. Now they know us everywhere. We did so many things on the show and your whole life can just change with one TV show. We would be in school now and doing our Leaving Cert, and just sitting there thinking about getting up and doing this, if we hadn't bothered.'

And Edward added that he and John would be very supportive of an Irish contestant who went on to win the show: 'I don't know if myself and John ever thought that we were going to win the show – we were just having so much fun from week to week. We weren't too sad when we got kicked off because it had been such a blast.

'I think it would be cool for someone from Ireland to win because there is awesome talent here. Everyone says it's because of you guys that Simon is coming to Dublin this year. If that was true, that would be amazing and Irish people should prove him wrong and go out there and win!'

Even though they are just about to turn 19, John and Edward are aware that they still have a very innocent outlook on life. The first time that Edward heard Katy Perry singing 'I Kissed a Girl', he thought that it was a little boy singing the song. 'That was the first moment when I realised that girls kiss girls,' he shrugs. 'Like, I don't know, that was kind of weird for me to find out.'

Both the boys are happy to be themselves and have no interest in the things that their peers getting into, such as going out to clubs and getting drunk. 'Before *The X Factor*, neither me or John had ever been inside a nightclub before and we didn't care,' says Edward. 'Going out and getting drunk shouldn't be seen as something that makes you cool and we don't need alcohol to make us cool. We could go to whatever clubs we want to now and probably not even have to queue or pay to get in, but we just have no interest in that type of thing. That's not what John and Edward are all about, and it never will be: we like the way we think.'

The morning of 4 July 2010 saw the twins getting up early in preparation for their performance at the T4 On the Beach festival in Somerset, England. They had their usual breakfast of cereal and fruit before leaving the hotel for the gig. Both were feeling confident and were keen to get on-stage in front of over 60,000 screaming fans at the festival.

All was going well and the boys were halfway through their 'Ghostbusters' theme tune when Edward landed badly on his knee and collapsed in agony. The brave twin immediately knew that something was wrong but continued with the performance, dragging his injured knee through the rest of the set.

At one point John dived into the crowd, while Edward remained on stage in obvious pain, but dancing and singing like a trooper. 'I think it was the worst pain that I have ever felt,' he admitted later. 'There were tears in my eyes but I didn't want to just lie there, I knew that John knew there was something wrong with me but I just wanted to get to the end. I didn't want to let the fans down or for us to have to stop – it was on TV and everything, there was just no way that I could stop.'

As their set drew to a close, the lads were helped off the stage, but Edward, writhing in agony, had to be carried by his minders. The unlucky twin was immediately rushed to a nearby hospital for x-rays on his knee.

Edward says that lots of people told him that his accident was worth more in terms of publicity than money could ever buy. 'Everyone left in a black car, but I left in an ambulance,' he says. 'The paramedics wanted to give me morphine and I was like, "No, I don't want morphine." They were like, "Take it," and I was like, "No, get away from me!"'

But his reluctance to take medication left the paramedics baffled as Edward was obviously in so much pain. 'Basically all the paramedics and people got together and they were like, I think we should be serious about this one.'

One fan did manage to get a picture of Edward in the ambulance, which was then sent out to all the newspapers in Ireland and the UK. Edward himself remembers the surreal feeling of everyone around him scrambling for photos and talking about what a good press story it was going to make but he was in extreme pain and knew that there was something very wrong with his knee.

'I was like, guys, I actually full-on hurt my leg – I'm serious, OK?' he recalls. 'The next day I saw myself in all the newspapers and it was like the world was coming to an

end. There was children dying in Africa and everything, and everyone was there talking about my leg.'

And in true showbiz fashion, the fall could not have come at a worse time. Jedward were just about to launch their début album in Ireland and the UK, and had a jam-packed diary for the next four weeks on the back of that. Promotional dates are vital for any group who are attempting to launch a new album so there's certainly no room for injury. And with John and Edward famed for jumping about on-stage with their high energy performance, Edward's injury could put the whole act in jeopardy.

Doctors soon gave him the news that everyone feared: he had ripped tendons in his knee and would have to stay off his leg for four weeks. But those four weeks just happened to be four of the most vital weeks in the lads' career.

John and Susanna flew over from Ireland to be at their son's side as he spent the night in a London hospital, devastated by the news that it would take four weeks to mend. But the next day, against doctors' wishes, Edward informed John that he would carry on, no matter how much pain he was in and that none of their performances were to be cancelled.

John commented: 'Jedward is a professional band. We have to go on for our fans.' Edward then admitted that he had 'cried like a baby' in pain after the fall – but only because he didn't want to let his fans down. The poor fellow was certain that Jedward were finished because of his badly timed mishap.

'It was the most painful thing that ever happened to me,' he admitted. 'I could hardly walk and I just thought that I needed to make it look like part of the routine. I think that John felt some of my pain because of the twin thing. I felt like I was leaving him to be a solo artist – and that's not what Jedward is about.

'I was crying like a baby in the ambulance, thinking that I have to do a tour of Ireland and promote the album.'

With further examination, Edward was told that he would need surgery on his knee, but he decided to put it off to continue with his Jedward commitments. 'Some people have told me that's silly, but I don't want to let the fans down,' he insisted. 'We can do the surgery when the time is right. Jedward is my No. 1 at the moment, and I want to give that everything and not let a pair of crutches get in the way.'

Doctors even warned him that he might never dance again if he didn't get specialist surgery on his knee, but still the defiant twin carried on.

The boys continued with their promotional work in England but had thankfully managed to shoot the video for 'All The Small Things' before Edward's accident. Jedward decided to channel a number of different looks in their second-ever video, which was recorded in London.

The opening shots see them with flat hair, black polo necks and silver winged runners and the boys drew inspiration from their favourite artists such Lady Gaga and Britney Spears to create the look. After scoring a No. 1 in Ireland and No. 2 in the UK charts with 'Ice Ice Baby', the duo were confident their second release could also be a hit.

In the second week in July 2010, Jedward dropped into Universal's offices in Dublin for a day of meetings with the press. It was just days until the launch of *Planet Jedward* and the twins were beside themselves with excitement. As well as filming for their ITV2 show, they were also being followed by an RTE crew for a second Jedward show due out in the fall.

The boys had just returned from a night in London, where they had an interesting encounter with some members of royalty. They admitted to being invited to dinner by members of the Qatar Royal family after meeting them at the Mayfair hotel and leaving female members in a tizzy. John revealed: 'The Royal family were in the same hotel that we were in and came over to talk to us. They took off their scarves that were covering their faces and we were told that they never do that. Their minders told us that some of them had never even heard them speak so that was cool. They told us to come and visit and go to dinner if we ever went there again. I think they had twins in the family, too.'

That night, Jedward were due to make sushi for manager Louis Walsh at their new apartment as part of their ITV2 show. Edward hinted that all was not going smoothly in their very first attempt to live away from home: 'John has broken a table and there was a bit of a flooding incident – we don't really know what we are doing. We are going to try to cook Louis dinner but we never cook, we just eat cereal. I think I can work a toaster.'

Just before the ITV2 show *Jedward – Let Loose* went to air, it emerged that the twins had caused over EUR15,000 of damage to their luxury apartment in Dublin. While living in the apartment for only nine days, John and

Edward managed to turn the place upside down in their first-ever attempt to live by themselves without anyone looking after them. The twins had never been left to fend for themselves without their parents or a minder to look after them and so the results speak for themselves. Neither of them had ever cooked, cleaned clothes or battled with day-to-day chores before being shoved into their own pad to look after themselves.

The hilarious footage shows Jedward trying to get to grips with the water system in the plush pad. And when they eventually figure out how to fill up the bath, they walk out of the room with water still flowing and forget about it. The result was complete and utter chaos as the bath overflowed and caused thousands of Euros worth of damage.

And the ITV crew who had been travelling with the lads refused to interfere in their mishaps so that viewers would get a real version of events. The producers, who were aware that the apartment was being flooded, had to wait for more than 40 minutes before the twins noticed what was happening. John and Edward also managed to break the hinges from doors and destroyed an expensive coffee table while messing around their new home.

Their first attempts to cook a meal were equally hilarious with Jedward setting off the fire alarm, even though they had been ordered to make a raw dish (sushi) that evening. ITV were left to foot the bill for damage to the apartment, but the documentary was a huge success and was also broadcast on TV3 in Ireland.

After the show, John admitted that he didn't know if he and his brother were ready to live by themselves just yet. 'There was lots of drama and we didn't even mean anything to happen, we were just hanging around and trying to cook dinner and stuff,' he said.

'The water was running and we went to see if it was working everywhere else and then we just kind of forgot all about it. When we went back in, we were like, oh my God! There was just water all over the place and we couldn't stop laughing. All of these things seem to just happen for us. We don't really know how to use a washing machine or anything but we are going to have to learn.

'Things just get broken around us – that has always happened. I think our mum was just glad that it wasn't all filmed in our house! I hope that landlords will still let us live in their houses, but maybe we could just buy our own place now.'

Ahead of the album release Jedward were booked up for TV and radio appearances all around Ireland. After one interview at the Today FM studio in Dublin, the lads were alarmed to be flashed by two fans waiting for them outside. The girls, who were filming for an online TV programme, sellotaped John and Edward's heads to their boobs before lifting up their tops as Jedward left the building. Ever polite, the boys averted their eyes, got into their car and sped off to the next appointment.

With the release of their very first album, *Planet Jedward*, in Ireland, 16 July was D-Day for Jedward. While John and Edward had an input in which tracks were picked for the record, the final decision was left in the hands of their manager and Universal. From the very start, Louis wanted Jedward to do an album of catchy covers. The lads had already perfected a number of hits while touring around Ireland with their solo show and all that was left for them to do was to get into the studio and lay down the tracks.

Naturally 'Ice Ice Baby' and 'All The Small Things' were included, but Louis had a hit list of other tunes that he wanted on the album. All the original artists in question had to be contacted by Absolute Records (a leg of Universal) and asked if they would give Jedward permission to cover their songs.

Although a few people turned them down, eventually the boys ended up with a stockpile of radio hits that were sure to satisfy the appetite of their fans. Their biggest coup was managing to get their favourite act – Backstreet Boys – to give the go-ahead for a recording of their hit single 'Everybody'.

Record company officials worked tirelessly against a tight deadline to ensure John and Edward were given the green light to re-record singles for their début release but the one number that the twins were really banking on getting was 'Everybody'. They didn't really care what song they got to do, so long as a Backstreet Boys' song was on their album.

John admitted that getting the go-ahead to record 'Everybody' was one of the highlights of the year for Jedward: 'When we were in the studio recording "Everybody", that was like a dream come true!' he said. 'If we closed our eyes, it was like we were in Backstreet Boys and back with them when they were doing it. We used to sing that song around our house and make up dance moves to go along with it, so when they said that we could do it, we were like, wow! I still love singing it – it's a brilliant pop tune.

'We got to meet them and nearly passed out because we were so excited. They played at the O2 in Dublin and Edward and I got to go along, and then we got a song. It's kind of like we are their follow-up band or something. I think that if we had been born earlier then maybe we could have been in the band because it's so us. They are heroes of ours.'

Also secured for the album was 'Ghostbusters' – the theme tune that Jedward had managed to bring to a brand new younger audience with their show-stopping performance on *The X Factor*. There was a strong 90's vibe with 'I Want Candy' and 'I Like to Move It' by Reel to Reel also featuring. The Robbie Williams' classic 'Rock DJ' that the lads had sung on the *X Factor Live* shows was also snapped up by execs to add to the line-up.

Even though their album was undoubtedly 'poptastic', Edward admitted that some people gave them guff for releasing a series of covers. 'I think the thing is that we were the first from the show to get a single out and the first to get an album out, and this is like a selection of our favourite songs,' he said. 'Everybody does covers and we sang lots of these on our tour so it felt right to put them on the album – we knew the fans loved them and that they wanted to dance to them. There was no way that we would have had time to write and record all of our own stuff in that short amount of time – we didn't even have that long to record them in the studio. But we do have some songs of our own. Maybe someday we can do those.'

Here is the final line-up for *Planet Jedward*:

'Under Pressure (Ice Ice Baby)' – 3:42 (Originally by David Bowie, Queen and Vanilla Ice)
'All the Small Things' – 2:53 (Originally by Blink 182)
'Everybody' – 2:53 (Originally by Backstreet Boys)
'Ghostbusters' – 2:54 (Originally by Ray Parker Jr.)
'Fight For Your Right (To Party!)' – 3:20 (Originally by The Beastie Boys)
'I Want Candy' – 3:15 (Originally by The Strangeloves)
'Jump' – 3:19 (Originally by Kris Kross)
'I Like to Move It' – 3:43 (Originally by Reel 2 Real)
'Rock DJ' – 4:03 (Originally by Robbie Williams)
'Teenage Kicks' – 2:22 (Originally by The Undertones)
'Pop Muzik' – 2:41 (Originally by M)

The decision was made to launch the album on 16 July at HMV in Dundrum Dublin – a shop that the twins regularly used to visit and buy CDs in when they were younger. The night before the launch, both John and Edward barely slept because they were too excited about the album hitting the shelves.

Fans had been gathering at HMV since the night before, with many taking the decision to camp out in the hope of getting a signed copy from the boys themselves. In an unprecedented move, the store was completely closed off from the front, as Jedmania took over. The 500 lucky fans who managed to get wristbands were the first allowed through the door to meet their idols.

As the twins took to their chairs at the top of the store, they finally got a glimpse of their very first album on the shelves. 'I think out of everything that has happened to us, this is the coolest!' Edward gushed. 'I mean, there we are – the album is on the shelf, the songs are playing on the background in HMV and the fans are all waiting to come in here and see us. This should be called Jedward Day from now on!'

The hard-working duo signed albums, T-shirts, arms, belly buttons and various other body parts for over 1,000 fans that day. Watched by RTE and ITV2 camera crews and record company execs from Universal, the boys continued to meet and greet tirelessly for hours.

Countless girls burst into tears upon meeting Jedward, with more than a couple having to be dragged away from them by Security. Some baked cakes, some brought sweets and others optimistically passed their phone numbers to an overwhelmed John and Edward.

Sixteen-year-old Janice Connolly, who had queued overnight to meet Jedward, declared: 'I'd love to go out with either of them. I gave them my number on a piece of paper. They signed my pillow and gave me a hug – it's just the best day of my life. Both of them are so nice and they remembered me from another time that I met them. I just can't decide which one of them is my favourite.'

Even after four hours of meeting and greeting fans, Jedward showed no sign of getting tired. John admitted that they didn't want to go home and leave some of their fans disappointed.

One photographer at the event revealed that he could remember when the boys themselves used to come along to signings at HMV and watch every move that the acts made. 'They were here for people like Westlife and other bands, and would always come up to photographers and try to get their picture taken,' he said. 'It's mad to think that they are here in their own right now with girls beating down the door, trying to get near them. All of the photographers in Ireland love snapping them, though – they are never in a bad mood and would do anything for you.'

The lads ran out of ink in their pens on a number of occasions and kept the waiting fans happy by jumping up and down in their cheers so that they could see them. Manager Louis Walsh also went to HMV Dundrum that afternoon to meet with his protégés and even though the fans were cheering for the pop manager, it was clear that Jedward were who they were really there to see.

Hundreds wore 'Jed-Heads' that had been specially created by the *Irish Sun* to commemorate the album's launch and Louis admitted he hadn't seen crowds like that since Boyzone mania gripped Ireland in the 1990s. 'You know, some people say that it's all about the Internet now and that people don't want to buy records, but today is proof that this is not the case,' he grinned. 'There are fans here who want that Jedward album on their shelves and they will listen to it until the CD won't work anymore. It's great to see!

'You don't see crowds like this for many bands these days or the kind of mayhem where girls just burst into tears – it's incredible and the boys will never want to leave. They just stay going like energiser bunnies until they meet all of the fans.'

And as Jedward tirelessly signed copies of their CD, they warned the next batch of X Factor hopefuls not to try and be like them. Edward insisted: 'Don't try to be like us. Everyone is looking to be the next Jedward this year but there is never going to be another one of us. People think that it's all about singing but it's not. We would not be sitting here now signing our first album if it was all about singing – it's not.

'No one should look over old shows and try to be like them: they should be unique. The reason that we are here today is because we were ourselves and never tried to be someone else. There never was a Jedward and there never will be another one of us, so if people are wondering how they can be sitting here next year, they have to be very different.'

Earlier that morning, the lads had caused mayhem at TV3's studios in Dublin when John jumped in on a live news broadcast: the boys were being filmed doing tricks with magician Keith Barry, but prankster John decided to take it to another level. Their tour manager Liam McKenna could only watch on in amusement as John jumped behind the journalist who was reading the sports bulletin and started to read out his lines.

The broadcaster was in stitches as John told him to continue reading out his lines and to 'be professional.' McKenna admitted: 'It was hilarious – live TV and John gets up there like that. The newsreader was trying to be serious but he just couldn't help laughing.'

John's unexpected stint as a sports journalist made it into all the national newspapers in Ireland the next day. Overall, it was a dream day in the lives of the Jedward twins, who then embarked on a nationwide visit of record store to sign *Planet Jedward* for more eager fans.

Just over one week later, the lads were celebrating the news that *Planet Jedward* had landed straight in at No. 1 in the Irish charts. The twins received a phone call from their manager Louis Walsh congratulating them and celebrated with a pillow fight. Edward said: 'This is like a dream and we don't want to sleep in case we wake up and it's not true. *Planet Jedward* is a bible that everyone should have – it's a bible of life.'

It was a major coup for Jedward, who managed to knock none other than Eminem off the top spot in the Irish charts. And given the fact that Eminem had just headlined the Oxegen Festival in Ireland the week before, replacing his comeback album *Recovery* at No. 1 was no small feat.

Louis admitted: 'It just goes to show how much the boys are loved over here. Eminem was No. 1 all over the world with that record and then Jedward came along. I wonder if he will be asking who they are now. John and Edward want to do a duet with him, so maybe that can happen now. It's a great pop record, full of great pop songs, and any kid out there would love it!'

The album managed to remain at the top of the charts for two weeks before being knocked off poll position by *The Suburbs* from Arcade Fire. Jedward could not have asked for a better start. In a time of ever-decreasing album sales and more online downloads, in 2010 the boys had managed to set a record for début album sales in one week in their home country.

It was a far cry from the days when Louis Walsh toured around Ireland buying up Boyzone CDs and putting them in the back of his car. The Jedward express had taken off all by itself and their Irish followers could not get enough of them.

A second nationwide tour was then announced to give fans around Ireland another chance to see their heroes live. And so the sun was shining and boy were John and Edward Grimes making hay!

Planet Jedward was also receiving positive reviews from music critics across the country, most of whom were of the opinion it was no masterpiece but the kids were going to love it. The album was to be launched in the UK on 26 July.

Jedward were still in celebratory mood and hit the town the night before their UK launch with Manchester United soccer hero Wayne Rooney. The twins spotted the footballing star during dinner at a top London hotel and John decided to ask him for an autograph. Rooney, who was there with his manager, then extended an invitation to the boys to join him for the night. Well behaved as ever, John and Edward sipped on water because their album was being launched the next morning.

Rooney extended an invitation to them to use his corporate box in Old Trafford anytime that they wanted it. 'He was really nice to us,' said John. 'We were walking out of the foyer and heard somebody shout, "Hey Jedward!" We turned around and it was Wayne. He asked us to hang out with him – he said our hair was cool. We hope to see him again soon: he's like the world's best player!'

The trio spent the night talking about Whitney Houston, the Beatles and football, while Wayne gave the youngsters some advice about coping with fame, telling them to keep their feet on the ground, stay focussed and be careful.

Even though *Planet Jedward* didn't top the charts in the UK, the boys were still delighted with the reviews they received from fans and critics alike. The album went in at No. 17 – a far cry from their top spot back home, but Jedward were undeterred. The boys had embarked on a gruelling promotional tour of the UK and made appearances on TV shows and radio stations all over.

'*Planet Jedward* got to No. 17, which isn't as good as Ireland but lots of the magazines and stuff said that they really like it,' said John, when asked about the performance of the album. 'We know that it takes time to build the foundations and just because you go straight in at No. 1 in Ireland doesn't mean that the same is going to happen in England. 'This just makes us want to make sure that our next album *is* No. 1.'

And the lads didn't let the fact that 'All The Small Things' hit No. 21 in the Irish charts and No. 80 in the UK charts get them down either. Edward shrugged: 'Our first-ever single was No. 1 here, you can't be at the top all of the time. We still love that song, though and we aren't going to stop singing it. Already we've had singles by Vanilla Ice and Blink 182 – even if Blink 182 ever heard our version, we would be so happy. They are so cool!'

While the twins went back to the UK on their hectic promotional schedule, Edward was still confined to the use of crutches. Stubbornly, he threw them away at every opportunity and walked around on his damaged leg. He admitted: 'I just hate them. We are so busy, and John is there jumping around and I just want to jump around. Every journalist seems to want to talk to me about my knee and I would rather just talk about Jedward.

'It's not as if my knee is the most important thing and it doesn't hurt that much. I don't want people to feel sorry for me: I'm fine. I love when reporters don't ask me about it – then everything feels like normal again. My crutches are cool, though. I knew that I would have to get different ones and we love gold, so then they got me gold ones. So now if I lose them people can just say, "Oh, they are Edward's" and then I can get them back.'

John and Susanna had arranged for him to meet with specialist surgeons at the Santry Sports Clinic in Dublin, who would decide what was best for his knee. Even though he was advised that he was going to need surgery as soon as possible, defiant Edward wanted to battle on until the lads had a break in their diary. He decided that he would undergo surgery in late August, when things were a little bit quieter in the land of the Jeds.

The boys wrapped their second Irish tour at the Waterfront in Belfast on 22 August before they were due a couple of days off. Edward was praying that he would have enough recovery time before a new tour was scheduled to kick off in the UK. Even though there was a break in their live touring, Jedward were still lined up for a string of TV appearances in Ireland and the UK, including Channel 4's *Alan Carr: Chatty Man* and *Loose Women* on ITV.

Tour manager Liam McKenna admitted that scheduling time to get Edward's knee sorted was nothing short of a nightmare: 'The thing was that he just did not want to cancel anything. So he was up there dancing away and giving it everything, night after night, and we were all worried about his injury. Eventually, he had to be told, "Look Edward, this has to be done."

'Time had to be cleared in the schedule so that no permanent damage was done. He was just so committed to doing everything that was in their diary and really didn't want to disappoint anyone.'

But there was more drama on the road for the accident-prone duo when Edward accidentally smacked John in the mouth with a microphone. While playing a date in Cork in August, he managed to slap his twin in the mouth and a tooth was chipped. John then had to make an appointment with his dentist to get the tooth capped when the band had a break.

Liam McKenna joked: 'God knows what else is going to

happen by the end of the tour! There seems to be one accident after another, but that's life on the road. With all the jumping about that the boys do, these things were bound to happen.'

Later that month, Jedward once again caught up with Vanilla Ice for a concert in County Wexford. The rapper was thrilled to be reunited with his pals back in Ireland and even admitted that he wanted to get a tattoo of them on his knees. While John and Edward considered returning the favour, they then had a change of heart.

'I think it's cool that Vanilla Ice was thinking about getting a Jedward tattoo,' Edward admitted. 'We were thinking that maybe we could get one to remind us of him, like a peace sign on our backs or something like that, but then we just changed our minds. That might get us in trouble with our parents.'

And the boys were beside themselves with excitement when Vanilla Ice then began texting his pal Britney Spears to tell her about them. 'I think me and John just couldn't really believe that was happening,' said Edward. 'Like for Britney Spears to even say our name – even on a text – I think that was just the coolest thing! He said that he would introduce us to her if we ever went to LA. I think we are going to have to go to LA, John!' he laughed.

Legendary rapper Vanilla Ice admitted that he was glad the twins had came along and his classic tune had been revived: 'Those two just have so much energy about them and I think that is really their secret – that is what is going to make them go far,' he observed. 'They are really good kids and I loved working with them. I didn't know who they were, and I looked them up on YouTube and the next thing you know, my song is all over the place again. It came at a good time and we all had a lot of fun with it, and I think it proved that the song can stand the test of time.'

At the end of July, John and Edward had discovered that they would be gracing the covers of legendary Irish rock bible *Hotpress*. The magazine, which previously featured the likes of Bono, Phil Lynott and The Frames on the cover, now wanted poptastic Jedward. But it came with a catch: the twins would go head-to-head with Snow Patrol singer Gary Lightbody for the special edition of a great Pop versus Rock showdown.

A spokesperson for the magazine said: 'The message is simple: If the Grimes make you grimace, then show your support for the rock cause and get the other issue. If you reckon that Jedward are the best thing since sliced pan and Gary Lightbody is indeed a tired pony, then get the Jedward issue.'

Jedward got off to a confident start, with Edward telling the publishers: 'It will be your biggest-selling issue.' The boys also told the magazine that they found it strange how girls who would never talk to them were now madly in love. John said: 'It's so weird because girls would never look at us before and now they are all like, "I love you". Normally when a guy wants a girlfriend, it's all about finding one girl to notice him but we have got thousands of girlfriends.'

And on 30 July the lads finally entered the *Big Brother*

house – but for one night only. The twins signed a lucrative deal, which meant they would appear on the last-ever series of the Channel 4 show and sing their new single 'All The Small Things', but the show's contestants were challenged not to react to strange events in the house for that week's shopping task: 'Ignore The Obvious'.

Jedward entered the House on Friday night and performed the single in the garden while the rest of the housemates struggled to ignore the strange events outside. *Big Brother* contestants had rushed to the doors as the partition to the garden was lifted up to reveal the twins performing outside.

Unable to ignore them, house mates Corin, Rachel and Andrew stood directly in front of the stage, watching Jedward perform. One contestant – Andrew – managed to avoid looking their way until Edward bounced off the stage and ran straight into him as he performed a dance move.

After their performance, the cheeky twins ran into the House and had a quick tour before they were asked to vacate the building by Big Brother. Not ones to leave on a quiet note, John and Edward set off the fire alarm before walking out.

Edward admitted: 'It was kind of crazy going in there. Deep down, they wanted to rock out with us, but they just couldn't. We set off the fire alarm, so they weren't very happy with us. It was really cool to be on the last-ever *Big Brother*, though.'

At the beginning of August 2010, the boys announced that they were finally ready to make a move into the fashion world. Having been signed by Next Models in

April and received offers to pose from *Vogue*, Jedward decided to capitalise on their fashion sense and chiselled good looks.

Ever since their very first audition in front of Simon, Cheryl, Louis and Dannii, their out-there but stylish fashion sense had captured the attention of everyone who tuned in to the show. And the pair had been working hard behind the scenes, coming up with sketches for their very own clothing label: 'Pop Icons'. Jedward admitted that they were looking to the very best for inspiration to design their clothes by checking out styles of icons such as Michael Jackson and Freddie Mercury.

John revealed that fashion was a huge passion for Jedward and added: 'our collection will look good on the catwalk.' The boys promised bold colours and 'cool patterns' as part of their début collection and revealed that manager Louis Walsh was in talks with a number of high street stores about selling their line of clothing.

Edward too admitted that they were feeling confident about their first venture into design and commented: 'We're signed to Next Models so we have experience. We know how to pose and walk plus, we have worked with some big-name photographers.'

Jedward had been dreaming about having their own clothing line since they were kids and stated that they hoped their new range could make them as wealthy as mega-rich Simon Cowell. The move into fashion was another attempt by the boy's management to show how versatile the Jedward brand could be and to keep them in the headlines.

In the first week of September 2010, John and Edward were enjoying a couple of days off in New York when they received some devastating news. Susanna phoned them to tell them that their beloved granddad Kevin had passed away in Dublin. Naturally, the boys were devastated and immediately organised a flight home.

When they got back to Dublin, the pair learned that they would be pallbearers at their grandfather's funeral and were happy to do so.

'He was an amazing person,' said John. 'We had been around him all of our lives and spent just as much time in our grandparents' house as we had at home – we couldn't believe it.'

And the boys did Kevin proud when they carried him to his final resting place at Esker cemetery, Lucan in early September. 'Only for our granddad, we might not have followed our dreams,' Edward admits. 'He always believed in us and was behind lots of the things we did. We were very close to him.'

As always in the world of showbiz, the show must go on and John and Edward were booked in for a huge TV appearance in Ireland just days after burying their grandfather. Even though Louis told them that they could take as much time off as they needed, the twins were keen to get the show back on the road.

Susanna and John travelled with them to RTE studios in Dublin to film the first in a new series of *The Late Late Show*. It was a serious coup for Jedward, who had last appeared on the show in November 2009 after leaving *The X Factor* and they would be going live in front of the Irish nation after host Ryan Tubridy had interviewed former British Prime Minister Tony Blair.

Never one to miss an opportunity, John and Edward caught up with Mr Blair backstage and asked him to pose with them for a picture – which he did. When asked by host Ryan Tubridy what they had thought of his interview with Blair, John answered: 'I'm serious, OK – that last interview was serious with a capital S.'

Jedward added that it had been an emotional week for them, with the death of both their beloved granddad and also their budgie, Joey. 'Our budgie died, and our Granddad died,' John revealed. 'We were real close to our granddad, and he always told us to follow our dreams and always told us that no star was too far to reach for.'

Edward also revealed that he was finally scheduled to have knee surgery the following week: 'Basically I hurt my leg, but I'm getting an operation next week and I'm really excited about it. They could like, start videotaping me. There's like real blood going everywhere and like, everyone's really scared.'

Their host also asked John and Edward what they thought about the recent revelations that auto-tuning had been used to alter some of the contestants' voices in the new series of *The X Factor*. They drew laughter of the crowd when Edward replied: 'They definitely didn't use that on us!'

As ever, Jedward stole the show and went on to hand out sweets to the audience members before a performance of their latest hit, 'All The Small Things'.

After spending the weekend with their family, it was back

over to London to film an entire series of *Celebrity Juice* in just one day. Then, on Friday, 10 September, time finally caught up with Edward and he had to go into hospital to have his leg sorted out.

Edward was booked into the Sports Injury Clinic in Santry, Dublin for the four-hour operation, which would repair the damage to the ligaments in his knee. Obviously experiencing nerves ahead of the operation, he confessed: 'I just hope that they don't find something else wrong with me while I am in there. Like one time I went to the dentist and he found this tooth that I wasn't meant to have.'

Not used to being apart, John had another bed put into Edward's private room so that he wouldn't have to spend the night alone. Edward was put under anaesthetic and four hours later, he woke from his surgery. Before he went into hospital, the twins had been planning on hitting LA for a few days while their schedule was cleared. But when Edward awoke drowsy and in pain after his surgery, he knew that it would be a different story and that he was going to need time to recover with the help of his mum.

'It was something that had to be done and I couldn't really put it off any longer, I suppose,' he admits. 'I didn't think that I was going to have to be on crutches for such a long time.'

Louis Walsh and Liam McKenna had managed to clear the twins' schedule for a week to allow Edward to recuperate, but the offers for appearances were still flooding in. Liam admitted: 'It's just nonstop and everyone wants them to do some work for them. There is barely a clear date in the diary between now and Christmas.

'Even at Christmas, they have gigs on Christmas Eve, Christmas Day off and then they are back to work on St Stephen's Day. They could be working 24/7, but it's important that they get enough rest or they will just burn out.'

Chapter Ten

going global with planet jedward

With a new series of *The X Factor* on the way, the twins would have to work harder than ever to ensure they remained in the limelight and that their star didn't begin to wane. With each series comes a new novelty act and as Cowell & Co. went in search of new stars for Series 7, many were saying that John and Edward's days were numbered.

And while some harsh critics in the UK were claiming that the bubble was already beginning to burst for the boys, they were still booked up for every day into 2011. Jedward would not be going anywhere, it seemed. With a brand new UK tour planned for November and a EUR100,000 role in *Cinderella* at Dublin's Olympia Theatre to look forward to, the boys were still very much in town.

John and Edward were thrilled to learn in August 2010 that Simon Cowell wanted them to appear back on *The X*

Factor for the live finals in the October. He extended an invitation to them to perform in front of the judges and live audience on the second night of the live finals. And Louis admits that his pal could scarcely believe that the twins were still around: 'I think people might have thought I was mad to take Jedward on but I knew what I was doing and a year on, here they are. They have the likeability factor, they have the X factor and Simon asking them back on proves that.

'Where are all the other people from the show? Most of them are gone back to their normal lives but John and Edward's lives will never be the same again and I am delighted for them. They are strong and tough and everything that you need to be to survive in this business.

'If they had cried and ran off stage the very first time they got booed, we probably would never have heard of them again – but they didn't. They stood up to everyone and now they are famous and millionaires.'

On Tuesday, 24 August, the first part of *Jedward: Let Loose* aired on ITV2. And the boys secured high ratings for their hilarious antics while living home alone for the first time in their lives. The documentary saw them left to their own devices for over one week in Dublin and the results made hilarious TV.

Asked what they had bought on their first shopping trip to the supermarket, the lads responded: 'We had to go to the supermarket ourselves for the first time on our own. We bought dog food, even though we didn't have a dog. We started tasting some of the food in the supermarket. We forgot to buy cleaning products and bin bags, and toilet paper and cups and plates, so our apartment got really messy.'

The wacky pair then went on to splash out on even more pet accessories to decorate their new home. Edward said this was simply because the pair have an eye for a bargain: 'I feel for me and John, it's always about getting a good deal and you could buy three dog cushions for the price of one normal cushion and we could give it to our dog when we were finished. And the dog bowls we bought are now used by our dog at home.'

As part of the programme, Jedward were also sent out speed dating in an attempt to find them girlfriends, but in typical Jedward style they ended up picking out the exact same girl. And John reckoned that she was 'one lucky girl' to get to go out with the two brothers at once: 'It was lots of fun and we had never done it before. We ended up picking the same girl, even though we talked to them all individually and then revealed to each other who we had picked. It just shows how alike we are and that we have the same taste in girls.

'We look for someone who is honest and cute and funny, and not wearing too much make-up. I think we do have the same taste in girls as we picked the same girl for our date.'

The twins admitted that the one thing they were looking forward to most about their own apartment was having a swimming pool, but it never happened. Also, the most they ever managed to cook up in the kitchen was a plate of toast and some cereal.

And then there was also a special appearance by soccer

ace Wayne Rooney's cousin Stephen, who showed off his tattoo of the twins. The 26-year-old showed John and Edward the tatt for the show and John exclaimed: 'Look, it's us!' Stephen also changed his middle name from Andrew to Jedward.

The boys later admitted that the worst thing about living in a new apartment as part of the documentary was that they had separate bedrooms. Edward revealed that he found it strange to have his own bedroom away from his twin: 'I think me and John as we are brothers have that bond that no one can separate us. We don't like being in separate rooms as we have no one to talk to and wake up, if we have nightmares.'

Jedward: Let Loose was also a huge ratings winner when it was shown on Irish channel TV3 one night after its ITV2 début. The second instalment of the show saw the lads attempt a shopping trip to IKEA to buy some 'essentials' for their new pad. The twins showed just how badly housetrained they were by snapping up random items such as LED lights and dog mats instead of essentials like towels and cutlery.

Mum Susanna asked road manager Liam McKenna to move in with the boys for the stay to keep an eye on them and perhaps it was a good job too. During their short stint in the apartment, John and Edward caused thousands of Euros worth of damage. Lights, tables and doors were broken as Jedward struggled to get used to life on their own.

And although they had started out in separate rooms, they soon moved their beds back together as they hated being separated. 'I think that as twins, they are just really close,' says Liam. 'Even though they were only across the room from one another, they didn't like to be apart. I don't think that it felt like home for them to be separated from one another.'

As already mentioned, one adventure that the boys went on for the programme was a speed date with 12 mystery Dublin girls. Here's what they had to say:

'I feel like they are going to cheat on me with you.'
'I feel like I am getting seconds.'
'If we were kissing, how would it work out? Do you want to try it out?'

With all the dates done, the boys got together to reveal their decision: both had picked the same girl – Caoimhseach. The thrilled wannabe actress admitted: 'I couldn't believe it, I was so happy!' And so the three sat down for a candlelit dinner at The Morgan Hotel in Dublin but lovestruck Caoimhseach was unable to pick out her favourite twin.

'The date went really well, it was really nice,' she enthused. 'They were just so fun.'

But neither John nor Edward was willing to go it alone and take her out, it seemed. 'We come first before girls,' John insisted. 'I feel like no girl could ever come between me and Edward. Jedmania is going to go strong – Jedmania has to continue.'

The final episode of the show centred round the boys' attempt to spend one night alone in the apartment. But when John and Susannah called round, the twins told them that they wouldn't mind if they stayed with them. While their dad sorted out the plumbing, Susannah pitched in and helped out with some cleaning around the apartment. John and Edward looked relieved to have them back after a couple of weeks of living by themselves.

And so the twins have yet to experience one full night alone without someone to look after them – something manager Liam McKenna is sure will happen sooner rather than later. 'It's going to have to happen,' he insists. 'One of these nights they are going to have to be left to fend for themselves and that is the best way that they are going to learn to look after themselves. They did really well living away from home for the first time, though and even manage to cook and entertain guests from the record company and wash some clothes. They came a long way in a relatively short space of time while the show was being made.'

The ITV2 series proved to be such a hit that John and Edward are due to speak with producers again regarding the making of another show. And it also turned out well for tour manager Liam, who was crowned *OK! Magazine*'s TV Hottie of the Week in Week Three.

Also in August, Jedward found out that they were in the running to have an Irish airport named after them. No-frills airline Ryanair issued a statement saying that the twins had topped a poll looking for new names for the brand new terminal at Dublin Airport. The Irish Government had hinted that a name change was a possibility and so Jedward fans got on the case and voted in their droves.

Ryanair's head of communications Stephen McNamara commented: 'Ryanair passengers have spoken and after over 10,000 votes were cast, Dublin Airport should now be renamed Dublin Jedward Airport – because its prices rise faster than their hair.'

Reacting to the press release, the twins posted a message on Twitter saying: 'If the airport is being named after us, we are going to be on tickets. Is everyone excited? We are. John Lennon is an airport in Liverpool, JFK is in New York and now Jedward Airport in Dublin.'

Ryanair polled the 10,000 passengers who chose Jedward from a field that included The Zoo and former Prime Minister Bertie Ahern. It's unlikely the name change will go in favour of Jedward, but as John and Edward have proved in the past year, nothing is impossible.

In September 2010, the twins recorded slots for *The Michael Ball Show* on ITV and another stint on *Chatty Man* with Alan Carr. They also appeared on *Sunrise* with Eamonn Holmes on *Sky News* to discuss their hairstyle and were requested by producers of *Loose Women*.

'I think it's cool that we get to be on these chat shows with politicians and different types of people,' John admits. 'Last week we were on *Alan Carr* and Whoopi Goldberg was there – I mean, how cool is that? We can talk to anyone about anything, though – we are cool and we don't get shy. We have met so many people in the last year and it's hard to remember them all, but we try to take as many pictures as possible and things like that because we might forget.'

Even though they have barely had a moment to

themselves, the twins insist that they are not getting tired of their gruelling schedule. When they do have an hour by themselves, however, the lads admit it is 'a luxury.' And when they do have downtime, John and Edward like to look up their old interview footage on YouTube and practise their dance moves.

Although they are adamant there is nothing else in the world that they would ever want to do, John admits that he once wanted to be an astronaut. 'I always wanted to get up high and go into space and find Planet Jedward,' he giggles.

The twins regularly find themselves working 19 hours a day, but say that it is worth it because they get to meet all of their fans. 'Fans are the main thing,' says John. 'They are so Jedicated and they buy your album.'

But every so often, being on the road does take its toll and the boys find themselves longing for their beds back home. 'The early mornings are sometimes tough because you get up at 5am and you just went to bed at 2am, and you always find yourself wishing that you had two more hours in bed or something like that,' Edward admits. 'Sometimes you miss your own bed and your own pillows because sometimes your bed isn't as comfy in a hotel as your bed at home.'

But the lads love taking in their surroundings while on the road and meeting new people in different towns all over the UK and Ireland. In just one year, John and Edward have toured Ireland three times over and at the time of press, they are about to take off on their first solo tour of the UK. And they can't believe their shows have been selling out every single night.

At first, the twins took all of their success in their stride, but now they are beginning to appreciate how well they have done to stay in the limelight. 'It is really cool that we can go out there and tour every night and sing to all of our fans,' John says. 'They scream our names and that's the most amazing thing in the world. When we were 4 and 5, we used to make stages in our house and put on these little shows, and now it is for real.

'We do know just how lucky we are and we want to start recording every minute of it so that we don't forget anything that is happening for us.'

Although John and Edward give off an air of being very independent and comfortable with travelling around, both have suffered from homesickness in the past. And even though they try to keep in contact with all of their family and friends as much as possible, the boys do get lonely on the road. The fact that they are also always losing their phones and computers doesn't help when it comes to staying in touch with their loved ones, but the twins try to phone home every couple of days and their parents can keep in touch with them by contacting tour manager Liam at any time.

John admits: 'We love meeting our friends, and bringing them on tour and backstage and stuff, if we haven't seen them for a while. It's really cool to show them everything that's happening. And it's nice to meet up with other pop stars too because they know what we are going through, too.'

And when the boys are not on tour, they are booked solid with endorsements, radio shows and TV appearances. 'We never have time off, but that's the way we like it,' Edward insists. 'We fill up our days with radio interviews and things, and then go out on-stage at night. You have to do as much as you can when you are out there and get as much information as possible out to your fans.'

At the end of the day, John and Edward's favourite way to relax is just to talk to one another or rent out a DVD. They also like to get out and play basketball/bowl or go running when they have a couple of hours to themselves. And another perk of now being famous is that they get an immediate backstage pass to see any bands that they want to.

John reveals: 'We love going to see our favourite groups now because we always looked up to them. It's really cool because sometimes you can get free tickets to go and see them now and we love that. And discovering new music is a really cool thing because we know how our fans feel when they listen to new music from us.'

John admits that he might not be so close to his twin, were it not for their shared passion for entertaining. He feels that their love of music has given them a close bond and brought them together more than any other interest they have: 'We have a really big respect for each other because we perform together as a group. It's the thing that we love the most and we look out for each other.'

But the boys admit their hectic schedule has played havoc with their diet. Gruelling stage appearances means that sometimes the twins won't get to eat until past midnight – something that concerns their mum Susanna. However, they stock up on sushi and grapes at every given opportunity and love nothing more than a midnight sushi feast. And their fans are also keen to make sure that they keep eating healthily by giving them food at signings.

Some bake cookies, others bake cakes and many bring the boys their favourite cereal and chewing gum. John and Edward always take time out to go through the stacks of presents that they have receive. 'One time a girl wrapped herself up as a present,' John laughs. 'She was trying not to move so that we wouldn't know that there was a person inside, but our fans always give us things that we really like. We even get clothes and socks and everything so we never really have to buy anything!'

As for the long-term future, neither of the twins likes to plan too far ahead. So many of their dreams have already been realised and it's hard for them to think about where they will be in ten years' time but both are firmly of the opinion that nothing is impossible.

With Louis Walsh's plans for global stardom, including careers in the US and Japan, the boys don't know when they will ever live at home again. 'I think that we do love to get home and get to our own bed, but we are kind of moving on from that all of the time,' Edward says. 'It would be really cool to like, live in LA under the Hollywood sign or something like that because we just love everything about America. No matter what happens, we will always be from Ireland and we will not forget our roots.'

The twins rarely spend a moment apart, but they know that the day may come when they want to go off, get married and have families of their own but neither can they ever see themselves living too far away from one another.

'That would just be too weird,' John shrugs. 'I don't think we would know what to do if we weren't near to one another because we have been beside each other for our whole lives.'

After nearly a year on the road, Jedward took some time out to reflect on everything that had changed in their lives. From unknown pop wannabes to *The X Factor*, a No.1 single and album and massive fame in just 12 months, John and Edward have experienced a lot of upheaval in their lives. Both are adamant that they would still be living in one another's pockets if *X Factor* had never happened, though.

'I think that we would just have done our Leaving Cert, and we would still be doing a lot of running and our lives would be the same as they were before all this, but we would still want to perform,' says John. 'Like, the thing about me and Edward is that if we wanted something, we always just wanted to go and get it. And people say it was destiny or meant to be, and that's kind of cool.

'I don't think that we have changed as people, though,' Edward adds. 'Like, when we go home to our dogs, they are still the same towards us. The year went by so fast and it was hard to take everything in, but it's there in video and documentaries and stuff, so that's cool. And the thing is, this is only the beginning: we are only 18 and have so much more to do.'

Both the boys have admitted they find it hard to keep in contact with their friends and family back home. They also confirmed that they had not met up with many of the *X Factor* contestants since the tour wrapped in April.

According to John: 'It's hard to keep in touch with everyone. We haven't really been in touch with anyone from the show. But we don't even really get to stay in touch with members of our family sometimes.'

'Our mum will be there giving out and telling us to call our granny and granddad,' Edward adds. 'They are our role models because they are really nice and really fun, and our favourite people to spend time with. We really miss our grandparents when we are away and try to call them as much as we can. I think they are proud of us, but they were always proud of us, even when we were just John and Edward goofing around at home. We always want to see them every time we go back to Ireland.

'It's not that we get lonely on the road because there are two of us but it's nice to see everyone, and everything is just normal and it's no big deal – it's like, eat your tea and put things in the dishwater. No one wants autographs in our family!'

The boys were on tour when they saw the front page headlines stating *X Factor* winner Joe McElderry had come out and admitted he was gay. Both insisted this was something that shouldn't matter in the world of showbiz.

'Joe decided to tell everyone and that is cool – loads of people are gay so it's no big deal,' Edward shrugs. 'I don't see why people make such a big deal out of things like that. He's a really cool person, and we are happy for him and hope that he is really happy.'

The boys insist they keep each other sane on the road and their unique bond as twins means they never tire of one another. Edward admits that his twin is the more focussed of the two and like a lead singer in a band: 'John is really the leader – he keeps me focussed. I tend to get distracted all of the time and John is like, "wake up, Edward!" One night I ate too many chocolate bars and he was asking me what the hell was I doing. He's a bit more sensible and I might be a little bit more laid-back and just sort of go with the flow.'

So, what's next for the prettiest boys in pop? Well, after their tour of the UK in November 2010, Jedward will be jetting into Ireland for their part as the fairy stepbrothers in the Christmas panto, *Cinderella*. The two-week run will see them net a hefty sum for their very first panto gig back in their hometown. And they can't wait to play their part in the shows that are already well on their way to breaking box-office panto records. This will be Jedward's acting début, but the twins have big plans ahead for their careers.

Both have admitted that they would love to play the part of James Bond and suggested dividing the role in two so that they could do half the work each. 'Maybe Simon Cowell could play the baddie?' John laughs. 'We could have like, an *X Factor* James Bond, with all of the characters being someone from the show.'

And Edward is confident the Jedward machine can keep on going until they are well into old age: 'Acting, singing, modelling... we can do all of those things so we are just going to go on and on, and keep our fans happy. They can tell us whatever they want us to do, we listen to them all of the time. I like to think that our fans are treated the best of all the fans in the world.'

And while John and Edward aspire to take over from

Bond, Louis Walsh also has huge plans for his most famous duo. The pop mogul wants to make them household names across the Atlantic and had already lined up meetings for the boys with agents in LA and New York back in August. And so the ball is rolling on getting them launched stateside.

'I reckon that by the middle of 2011, people in the States are going to be talking about John and Edward. We have big plans for both of them,' Louis grins. 'If they think that 2009 and 2010 were amazing – well, they haven't seen anything yet! America is where they could really make it and I think that they will be lapped up over there.

'It's brilliant because everyone thought that these boys weren't going to last and look at them now. They are great, they are terrific ambassadors for Ireland, they are fun and girls love them. I think America is going to go crazy for them. The Jedward story is just getting started.'

Indeed, when John and Edward visited America at the start of September 2010, they were recognised by people from all over the world, who had came across them on the Internet. And still showing the same steely determination that made them famous in the first place, they dressed to the nines and went out looking for tickets to top TV shows being recorded in New York in the hope of building up their profile.

The sad passing of granddad Kevin meant that they had to come home early, but there's no doubt about it, the twins' onslaught on the US is only beginning and they won't so much as take an unscheduled day off just in case it has all been one big dream.

Even though they have spent practically every day for

close to 18 years together, the twins insist they have never fallen out. Edward reckons this is because if they did fight, they would be stuck for someone else to talk to. 'It's just the two of us most of the time and we are always together, so we can't really fight' he reveals. 'If there is ever a moment we just tell each other to get real and that we aren't in some sort of drama series.'

John and Edward have even come across some people who claim their close relationship as brothers must be some sort of act for TV, but John insists: 'That's just the most ridiculous thing ever! We are each other's favourite people and we act the same with each other, whether there are people in the room or not. If you put hidden cameras on the two of us, then we would just act the same – we aren't like other celebs who are all fake.'

'John never annoys me,' Edward adds. 'We never get angry with each other and always just want each other to do better. If I'm eating like, a packet of cookies, then John will go, "No, Edward!" and show me a picture of Zac Efron and go, "This is where you need to be at."'

It seems the duo are happy to continue working with each other forever. Edward said: 'It's hard to have people that you can trust around you but I feel that right now, we have the right team. If you don't have the right people around you, then you are not going to get anywhere. Like, if there was anyone around us that thought we weren't going to make it in America or something then we would have to get rid of them. Say someone said like, I looked horrendous and John said I looked amazing I would go with John's opinion because he knows me best.

'We want to start keeping a diary of everything that happens us now so that we can show our grandkids and we would want them to just go out there and follow their dreams too.'

One thing that they are sure about, however, is that they are not ready for serious girlfriends or marriage yet. John says: 'I find that sometimes... OK, me and Edward have all these girls throwing themselves at us and they totally love us. They want to have our baby, it's crazy – think how innocent me and Edward are, OK? We love Taylor Swift and girls who don't wear all of this make-up, and who know who they are and are cool.'

'Yeah, we want girls who make us look manly,' Edward adds.

And as for the year ahead, John and Edward have big plans. In 2011, they both want to get involved in the production side of their shows and take their tour to places where they have not yet been. As well as new albums and more single releases, the boys are also keen to start working on writing some songs once they get a bit more time to themselves.

'I think we want huge stages and huge productions – bigger than anything anyone has ever seen us do before,' Edward reveals. 'We have so many ideas about things that we want and we love to get our ideas out there. We have learned about controlling the crowd and want to make everything better and better with every tour.'

They are also planning to release a number of new books, including one made up of photos of them from their time in the limelight. John hopes neither he nor his twin will ever tire of performing. He says: 'It really is something that we are planning on doing for the rest of our lives, but if one of us gets bored with it then we are going to have to deal with that. But right now everything is really different every day and so that keeps it all fresh and we love it.'

The fun factor is something both boys are keen to keep in their daily schedule and they never want to take their fame for granted. The fact that they consider their fans to be their friends means that they never want to lose them. Some Jedward fans have become very close to the twins and they know them on a first name basis. The twins say that one of their golden rules is that they are never rude to, or ignore a group of fans. Edward stresses he and John will always say hello and be kind to their fans because, 'they got us where we are today and they make us the coolest things in the world.'

In September 2010, John and Edward were named the faces of Nintendo. As part of their lucrative new deal, the twins received computer games and loads of accessories. And although they get free merchandise, shoes and clothes sent to them all of the time, the lads say the best thing about being famous is getting to meet their fans.

'I think that the coolest thing about being famous is that you get to meet your fans and to go all of these cool places,' Edward says. 'When you are happiest, nothing can change what you are thinking of. I think that if we weren't pop stars then maybe we could be a pirate on a ship. Our favourite musician who has been the favourite person we have met has been Paul McCartney.

Looking to the future, he continues: 'Me and John, we

want to travel the whole world and go to every single country that we can. I have a dream that one day, John and Edward can walk down the street with their hair spiked up and not have someone go, "Why is your hair spiky?" One day, everyone will know that spiky hair is cool.'

John adds: 'You know what guys, believe it or not but it only takes me a couple of seconds to do my hair in the morning with gel. When I do it with a hair-dryer, it takes me less than five minutes. I just dump a load of crap in it and see what happens!'

At a photo call to launch their upcoming role in *Cinderella* at the Olympia Theatre in Dublin, both boys admitted that they are scared to take a holiday in case their fans feel abandoned. Since auditioning for *X Factor* in 2009, Jedward have had just a handful of days off, but their manager Louis Walsh reckons the duo will soon learn how to relax. He says: 'When something happens this fast for people, they are afraid to go away in case the bubble bursts. I have told Jedward to take time off, but they don't want it and they have never asked for it. I think they wanted to be famous for so long and now that they are, well they understandably never want it to end.

'I hope that they don't burn themselves out, but they are fit and look after themselves and don't party so they can just stay going. They have more energy than anyone else that came from *X Factor* last year and that is why they are so successful.'

The boys used to enjoy school trips and family holidays to Italy and Tunisia, but will now settle for a quiet night at home with their family. John says that they have no desire to head off to a sunny island for a luxury holiday when there is still work for them here: 'If we were gone I think we would just be wondering what we could have been doing with Jedward at the same time. We are always on planes and always travelling anyway, so we don't need to do that.

'If we take a holiday then it might all stop and we don't want fans to forget us: I think that they would miss us if we went away and we would miss them too. We want to be here, where it's happening and are always really hard on ourselves because we want to do better. We always forget about everything that we have achieved and just restart ourselves.'

Edward is a firm believer that they both need to work hard to ensure the fans that they have remain fans for life: 'We don't want to be a fad, we want to be around forever. If your fans don't know where you are gone to, then you are going to lose them. They have dedicated their lives to us and we just want to do the same for them, really.'

For now, John and Edward must wait on Edward's leg to recover while preparing for dates in Ireland and the UK in October and November 2010. This will be their fourth time to have dates in Ireland in just one year, but their first UK tour without the rest of the *X Factor* crew. And they are licking their lips at the chance of getting on the road for a full month and seeing all of their UK fans.

'This will be the first time that they can come and see our solo shows, and we are going to make them really special,' Edward says. 'The thing about me and John is that we are learning as we go along and already we have learnt so much in a year. We were full of ideas for the UK tour because we had already toured Ireland a couple of times, so I really hope that the people there are blown away.'

Overall, 2010 has been a whirlwind year for John and Edward: No.1 albums and singles mixed with the passing of their grandfather all make for an emotional rollercoaster, but Jedward are surrounded by a top-class team, who are always on the lookout for their welfare.

The Irish twins were supposed to be just a 'flash-in-the-pan act' but they have gone on to prove an awful lot of people very wrong. A packed diary, fashion line, new music and countless TV appearances means one thing is for sure: the Grimes Brothers won't be going anywhere in 2011, either.

This is one party that is just getting started.

quotable quotes

Cheryl: Where do you see yourself in 15 years from now?
John: Well, I see myself as being older.

John: We've got our *Ghostbusters* gun! I was expecting a lot bigger but you know, it does the job... It has the beam: it kills the ghost...

John: We naturally stand like this.
Edward: No, we were asked to stand like this. But I don't want to stand on the left for the rest of my life – you know, what's going on, on the right? Maybe one day...

Interviewer: And suddenly you were being portrayed as the villains. Did it feel that way to you?
John: I don't know, 'cause we were being portrayed.
Edward [points at John]: Does this look like a villain?

John: No.

John: I'm John, I'm Edward – peace out!
Edward: *I'm* Edward!

John: Our favourite colour is blue.
Edward: Black. Black-blue.
John: We both love black-blue.
Edward: You don't! You don't even like black...

John: We're going on a red carpet! Not a blue, not a purple... a red carpet.

Edward: Once I was like, 'Look, John, that's you on TV!' Then I realised it was me.

John: What's my favourite part of the song? Erm... 'Oops!... I did it again' 'cause it's kinda like, I did something bad and I didn't ask permission but I go 'Oops, I did it again' and everyone's like, 'Oh, it's OK, he said, oops I did it again...' So, yeah.
Hairdresser: [starts laughing]
John: As you can see, the hairdresser is not taking her job very seriously – she's laughing when she should not be laughing. But I don't know what's so funny.

Holly Willoughby: Do you just wake up and your hair's like that? Do you have to sleep upside down or something?
Edward: It's a secret, guys, OK?

John: When people were going 'Boo!' I think that they could have been going 'Wooooo!'
Edward: I think it's just, like, part of our act – it's like, people go, 'Oh my God, it's John and Edward! Let's boo!'

[Talking about their performances]
Edward: I think it's better to hype it up more – like the bigger, the better.
John: Well, it wasn't *that* big.
Holly Willoughby: So, you want more?
Edward: Yeah, let's get lions.

John: Edward, why are you wearing that T-shirt? You're not on team Simon.
Edward: I'm on team Simon, OK? Get over it!

Interviewer: What's your favourite type of monkey?
John: Er... chimpanzee.
Edward: Whatever it was, I didn't do it. OK?
Interviewer: Yes, but what's your favourite type of monkey?
Edward: Oh, the yellow one.

Edward: Just like people think that Justin Timberlake invented the suit, he didn't invent the suit. And me and John didn't invent spiky hair but we went with it and now we totally own it.

On *This Morning*:
Philip Schofield: So, what's the plan? What will you do now?

John: 'Well right now we're doing *This Morning*.

Edward: My chewing gum's nearly chewed.

John: No girl would ever come between me and Edward. If they tried, we would tell them to go away.

Edward: We met Alexandra Burke the other day. We said: 'You're cool, we are bad boys!'

Edward: We just want to give a big shoutout to our granddad, who owns a tractor.

John: If Edward gets ill, I do too. So, we'll both stay off school. There's no point in me going in. What's John without Edward?

Edward: Sometimes people come and say, 'I like you better than John.' I'm like, 'Don't say that!'

Edward: Me and John's hair was never an intentional thing but now that we think about it, it is really, really cool that our hair is actually the way it is. When people see us, they don't need to look at our face. Girls usually go 'stop looking down there, our face is up here!' We go, 'Stop looking up there, our face is down here!'

John: People usually don't know who to look at when they are doing interviews. When I listen to Edward, it freaks him out.

Edward: We were on the *Blue Peter* show and we had to do another retake of the show because John said a bad word.

John: We are like the Bill Gates of spiky hair.

Edward: We love Joan Rivers because she's really cool. Ellen and Oprah are really cool too and we want to get on their shows – Ellen especially because I want to dance on her table!

John: We used to go to the movies, and get popcorn and things. I think everyone has that moment in the cinema where they drop all of their popcorn. I remember dropping all of the popcorn but it didn't actually land on the ground – it landed on this lady's head in front of us and she wasn't very happy.

Edward: I remember our next-door neighbours had mint plants and me and John used to go next door and eat them. And then we would mix it with chewing gum to make it mintier. The people next door thought that the mint plant had like, flies or something but actually it was just us.

Edward on John:
✦'John is totally innocent and he would never want to hurt anyone.'
✦'John is basically my representative and anything he says goes for me too.'

★'Sometimes he can get shy and not many people know that.'

★'Sometimes I don't know how he would be without me because I can talk instead of him.'

★'He's really driven – he's like a car and likes to drive places and get things done.'

★'John doesn't like mean girls and only likes sweet ones.'

★'He likes girls who look like Lindsay Lohan and doesn't like the fact that there's girls out there who think that they are hot when they are not.'

★'It's hard to describe him without describing myself but the big difference between us is that... I don't know, there actually is no difference.'

★'We are like two scientific experiments and you end up with the same results.'

John on Edward:

★'I think with girls, Edward would look for honesty and someone who is sensitive and someone who is funny and can make you laugh. Like me, he would want a girl who knows herself and can do her own thing, and then let me go to do my own thing – it's all about being a nice person.'

★'Edward is a really nice person.'

★'Some people might think that he is like, the quiet one, but he isn't really at all.'

★'He is the person that I go to for everything and we don't really like when we are away from one another.'

★'I would say that Edward is a bit more messy than me and sometimes might eat more junk, and I have to say,

"Hey, you are a pop star – you can't do that!" and he just laughs.'

★'I think that Edward is happiest when he is onstage or with our fans, just chatting. Oh, and he's also happiest when he is eating sushi and his hair is perfect!'

★'We just cut our own [hair] most of the time now because we still don't like the thought of hairdressers running around after us with their scissors.'

★'As corny as it sounds, the best thing ever to happen for me and Edward is when fans started to ask us for autographs.'